Cincinnati
Reds
Legends

S. Hannig

Cincinnati Reds Legends

Mike Shannon

Illustrated by Chris Felix, Scott Hannig, and Donnie Pollard

Black Squirrel Books™ 🐿 ™

Kent, Ohio 44242

Frontis: Shortstop Roy McMillan. Illustration by Scott Hannig.

Text copyright © 2015 by Michael Shannon
Illustrations copyright © 2015 by Chris Felix, Scott Hannig, and Donnie Pollard
Foreword copyright © 2015 by The Kent State University Press, Kent, Ohio
All rights reserved
ISBN 978-1-60635-231-1
Manufactured in China

BLACK SQUIRREL BOOKS™ 🐿️™
Frisky, industrious black squirrels are a familiar sight on the Kent State
University campus and the inspiration for Black Squirrel Books™, a trade
imprint of The Kent State University Press.
www.KentStateUniversityPress.com

Cataloging information for this title is available at the Library of Congress.

19 18 17 16 15   5 4 3 2 1

Contents

Foreword

When I first began writing about baseball and the Cincinnati Reds in the mid-1980s, I came across the name Mike Shannon. As in, "You gotta meet Mike Shannon." "You should get together with Mike Shannon." As I soon learned, introductions to Mike almost always came with a disclaimer: "Not the Mike Shannon Who Played for the Cardinals," but the other Mike Shannon, the *writer* Mike Shannon.

By the time I met Mike he was a cottage industry. He wrote baseball books (which at that point in my career was really cool, since I hadn't come close to completing one). He was an editor of a baseball literary magazine that he founded. He was a contributor to journals and other baseball publications and the host of an annual banquet that presented the Casey Award (another of his offspring) to the author of the best baseball book of the year. Mike himself seemed to be working on three books at once: the one he had just published and was promoting, the one he was in the middle of writing, and next one he was going to write. Mike seemed to know everybody in baseball publishing. He had the grandest baseball library I had ever seen. The Casey Award banquet always attracted a big-time writer or two. Mike was sort of the George Plimpton of Cincinnati sports writers, a one-man baseball salon.

His literary publication, *Spitball Magazine,* was his brainchild (along with the late Jim Harrison). At various points an annual, a semi-annual, or a quarterly (depending on submissions and the shoestring budget), *Spitball* was one of the few venues for serious baseball writers, be they poets or essayists. The magazine included book reviews. It featured original art on the cover and illustrations scattered through the pages. Mike always liked baseball art.

And in this new book, *Cincinnati Reds Legends: The Greatest Players of All Time,* it is the art that shines. Over the years, Mike has showcased a number of baseball artists in his various projects and three of them are featured in this book: Chris Felix, Scott Hannig, and Donnie

Greg Rhodes

Cincinnati Reds Team Historian

Pollard, familiar names if you have followed Mike's work over the years.

Mike has picked the 40 greatest Reds players (and yes, we can argue around the margins about who was left in and who was left out, but this really isn't a book that wants to argue). Nearly every decade is represented. All the obvious choices are here; I'd be surprised if your favorite Red isn't included. Mike has written succinct and interesting biographies, mixing in popular details with lesser-known stories. It isn't easy, I can attest, to write engaging bios about such renowned players.

Forty greatest Reds players and 40 Mike Shannon profiles make for an interesting book in and of itself, but I don't think Mike will mind if I lavish the highest praise on the artists. As Mike said, "Art is going to carry this book," and he couldn't be more correct, nor could he have picked better artists. All three deliver outstanding images, page after page. Compelling forms, colors, compositions. Many of the illustrations draw their inspiration from photos but transcend the photographic image by conveying the artful essence of the strength or reputation of each player. You can feel the power in the George Foster swing, the incredible presence of Sean Casey, the concentration of Bubbles Hargrave, the dominance of Johnny Bench.

Over the years, Mike has written nearly two dozen baseball books; I would submit this will be his best. As the founder of the Casey Award, Mike has declared himself ineligible for the annual prize. With this book, he should reconsider. It would be a shame not to include what will surely be one of the prized books of the year from the competition. At the very least, I will be happy to nominate *Cincinnati Reds Legends: The Greatest Players of All Time,* for the literature wing of the Reds Hall of Fame.

Buy it, enjoy it. Find a picture to hang on the wall. Thanks, Mike, Chris, Scott, and Donnie for a masterpiece.

Introduction

Despite appearances to the contrary, I have not been a lifelong Reds' fan. I grew up in Jacksonville, Florida, which was Atlanta Braves' territory, if anything; but I was a San Francisco Giants' devotee . . . because of Willie Mays. Yet I'm a big Reds' fan now, my destiny having brought me as a young man to Cincinnati, where the culture and the history of the place slowly insinuated itself into my blood and consciousness—especially the fascinating and glorious history of the city's professional baseball team. Cincinnati feels like home now; Jacksonville, a nice place to visit where relatives still live.

I arrived in the area just in time to see the last gasp of the Big Red Machine. I lived in Covington, started a literary baseball magazine there with a dear friend, now gone, and used to walk across the Roebling Suspension Bridge to watch Reds' games in a ballpark that became as familiar as an old friend, Riverfront Stadium, also now no longer with us.

I missed Crosley Field and Frank Robinson and before him Ted Kluszewski and before him Edd Roush, who played for the Reds before I was even born. But I have gotten to witness a lot of Reds' history. I was at Riverfront the night Johnny Bench hit a home run to pass Yogi Berra; I was there on the night Bench retired, when he hit the final home run of his career; and I was there, with my one-year-old son, Mickey, sitting on my lap, when Pete Rose slapped a single into left field to pass Ty Cobb. I think I was also on hand for Rose's return from Canadian exile, but I'm not sure about that, even though I have a crystal-clear memory of him sliding headfirst into third base, as he stretched a double into a triple and brought hope for better days back to Reds' fans everywhere.

The truth is that I can "remember" a lot of Reds' history that I definitely wasn't present for because I've spent the past three decades reading about it, conversing about it, dreaming about it, and writing about it. Reds' history is like that. It's so exciting, so interesting, so vivid that it becomes your history too.

This book is about 40 of the Reds' greatest players. My colleagues and I will be happy if, after reading it and soaking in the images, you "remember" watching them all play—even the ones who earned their glory long before you came into this world.

Don't think for a second that we didn't agonize over the selection process for the book's roster. We are the first to admit that worthy players got left out; it was inevitable. Yet if you read and look carefully, each subject's qualifications as a "Legend" of Reds' baseball should be apparent. If you want to tell us whom we shouldn't have left out, you also have to say which included player you'd take off the team.

I hated to see the writing of this book come to an end because for six months I have lived alongside these great Reds' players in the Cincinnati dugouts, grandstands, clubhouses, and press boxes of the past.

As I said, I didn't grow up a Reds' fan. But my beautiful wife of 35 years, Kathy Dermody, wasn't my first girlfriend either. And I found her in Cincinnati too.

It has been a privilege to work with the three artists whose brilliant work illustrates the book, and I extend my sincere thanks to them for their hard work and dedication. The four of us thank the professionals at The Kent State University Press, particularly director Will Underwood and marketing manager Susan Cash, for their guidance and enthusiasm.

MIKE SHANNON
February 2014, Cincinnati, Ohio
Ad majorem Dei gloriam

1869–1925

Harry and George Wright

Entire books have been written about the numerous threads that were woven together to create the wonderful tapestry that is the game of baseball. Many a pioneer had a hand in the development of America's national pastime, but there were none so important as two cricket-playing brothers who became the heart and soul of the game's first professional team, the legendary Cincinnati Red Stockings of 1869.

Harry Wright, born in Sheffield, England, on January 1, 1835, came to America around the age of 10 when his father, Sam, was hired to be the cricket professional at St. George Cricket Club in New York. Harry played cricket too but, to the chagrin of his father, became enamored of the new American game "base ball," as did younger brother, George, who was born in Yonkers.

Harry played baseball in 1858 with the famous New York Knickerbockers when the game was the province of amateur gentlemen. By the time he moved to Cincinnati in 1865 to teach cricket, many "amateur" baseball players were getting paid under the table. When the Cincinnati Red Stockings club wanted a manager to find "the best men procurable" to play on the first openly professional, salaried baseball team, they hired Harry Wright. The first player Harry hired was the best shortstop in the country, his brother, George.

Harry drilled his handpicked Red Stockings club in the fundamentals and exerted an avuncular but firm discipline over his players. The team toured the country, completed a perfect 57–0 season, and captured the nominal national championship, repeatedly sending their supporters into frenzies. Cincinnati's June 15 win over the Mutuals in New York by the uncharacteristically low score of 4–2 was hailed as the greatest game of ball ever played. The best "striker" on the team was George, who batted .633 and scored 339 runs in 480 at bats. Harry played center field and batted .493.

The Red Stockings won another 24 straight games to start the 1870 season; but things were different, as other teams followed Cincinnati's lead and declared themselves professional outfits. The Red Stockings finally lost a game on June 14 to the Brooklyn Atlantics, 8–7, crushing their supporters, who reacted as if they expected the team to never lose. The team finished 67–6, giving them a two-year record of 124–6. Superlative, but not enough to preserve the club. Rowdy behavior by second baseman Charlie Sweasy, jealousy over the Wrights' higher pay, poor attendance, and the considered-to-be excessive salary demands of the players caused the officials of the club to disband it. Although Cincinnati did not field another pro team until it joined the fledgling National League in 1876, the Red Stockings of 1869–70 gave their modern descendants an unrivaled heritage and ignited a torrid love between the city and the game, which has never waned.

Harry and George both went on to have long, successful careers in the first professional baseball leagues. Under Harry's leadership Boston finished first in four (1872–75) of the five seasons that the National Association lasted, and he then won two (1877–78) of the first three National League pennants. In all, the "Father of Baseball" managed 2,145 games and compiled a 1225–885 record. Harry went to his grave with the admiration of everyone who'd ever known him, and the year after he died (1895) cities around the country played games to raise money to build a monument in his honor.

As for the "King of Shortstops," George hit well for his brother in Boston (.388 in 1873) until the faster and curved pitching of the National League (NL) slowed him down. After baseball he started a sporting goods business and helped introduce other new sports, such as golf and hockey, to America.

GEORGE WRIGHT											
YEAR	TM	G	AB	R	H	HR	RBI	SB	BB	SO	BA
1871–75	BOS (5 yrs)	262	1379	401	483	9	194	47	25	16	.350
1876–78 1880–81	BSN (5 yrs)	198	921	171	246	1	81	-	26	47	.267
1879, 1882	PRO (2 yrs)	131	573	93	137	1	51	1	17	56	.239
Total		591	2873	665	866	11	326	48	68	119	.301

Will White

His records are not recognized because he played in the nineteenth century when the rules of the game as we know it today were still evolving. Yet, the records set by William Henry White are amazing, and no list of Cincinnati Reds' legends would be complete without this fascinating pioneer, the team's first great pitcher to participate in league play.

Will White was born in Caton, New York, and grew up on a farm with his older brother. Nicknamed "Deacon," Jim White would become a star catcher and eventually be inducted into the National Baseball Hall of Fame. Will was a pitcher and got his first taste of fast play with independent Binghamton in 1876. The next year Will and Deacon joined the Boston club of the newly formed National League, and the two became the first brother battery in pro baseball history. Will pitched in only three games, but all three were against the Cincinnati club, which signed the brothers for the 1878 season.

Will led the Reds to a second-place finish in '78 with 30 wins, an ERA of 1.79, and the second-most strikeouts in the league (169). This stellar work was just a warm-up for his impressive encore. In 1879 White started 76 games, completed 75 of them, and pitched a total of 680 innings, all major-league records. He finished second in the league in wins with 43 (against 31 defeats) and in ERA (1.99). Although pitchers threw underhanded at the time, White's ironman work in '79 still amounted to an epic performance.

White was the first pro player to wear spectacles, and fans today may gaze upon photos of him with those rimless glasses, his walrus mustache, and thinning head of hair and figure him as some sort of nonathletic milquetoast. White did follow gentlemanly pursuits away from the diamond: he owned and operated a tea shop, a grocery, and a drugstore in Cincinnati, and after baseball he took up songwriting, penning a ditty called "Little Puff of Smoke, Good Night" for which Ring Lardner supplied the lyrics. But he was no pansy on the field. He was a battler who took delight in plunking batters with his pitches and then yelling "Whoop-La," which became one of his nicknames (he was also known as "Medicine Bill"). He was enough of a menace that the American Association (AA) instituted the "free base for a hit-by-pitch" rule specifically to curb his intimidating tactic.

In 1881 the Reds were kicked out of the National League for selling beer at their games, and White basically sat out the season, his one-month tenure with Detroit a halfhearted effort. When the upstart American Association formed a year later, White was one of the first players signed by the Reds' entry.

The Reds captured the AA's first pennant in 1882 behind their ace hurler, Will White. He led the league in wins (40), complete games (52), innings pitched (480), and shutouts (8). In 1883 he won a league-leading 43 games—the third time he'd topped 40 wins in a season—and he also led the Association in ERA (2.09) and shutouts (6) again.

White was named captain of the Reds for the 1884 campaign, but he was neither popular nor effective in that leadership role. Considered a fast pitcher in his younger days, White refused to adopt the new overhand style of pitching that was catching on, and the hitters quickly caught up to the slower pace of his offerings. He finished with 229 wins, all but two earned in a Reds' uniform. He ran his grocery in Cincinnati for a while but eventually moved to Buffalo and drowned in 1911 while teaching a niece to swim.

Year	Tm	W	L	ERA	GS	CG	SHO	IP	H	R	BB	SO
1877	BSN (1 yr)	2	1	3.00	3	3	1	27	27	15	2	7
1878–80 1882–86	CIN (8 yrs)	227	163	2.26	396	389	35	3497.2	3389	1811	492	1029
1881	DTN (1 yr)	0	2	5.00	2	2	0	18	24	18	2	5
Total		229	166	2.28	401	394	36	3542.2	3440	1844	496	1041

Bid McPhee

The Cincinnati Reds, who proudly claim a number of "firsts" in baseball history, also boast a significant "last" in the person of John Alexander McPhee. The son of a saddle maker, McPhee ironically disdained the use of leather while playing second base until long after fielders' gloves had become commonplace. "I have never seen the necessity of wearing one; I cannot hold a thrown ball if there is anything on my hands," he said when asked why he didn't use a glove. Not until 1896, in the 15th year of his 18-season career, did McPhee, who soaked his hands in brine every spring to toughen them, deign to wear a glove; and he relented then primarily to help himself recover from a broken finger. All he did that year was shatter the previous mark for fielding percentage by 19 points. Well before that watershed year though, McPhee had established himself as the best fielding player of the nineteenth century, a time when being able to "pick it" was much more important than it is today.

Born November 1, 1859, in Massena, New York, young "Bid," as McPhee was called because of his small stature, played a few seasons of minor league ball in Davenport, Iowa, and Toledo, Ohio, and then contemplated retiring to work full-time as an accountant. The Reds of the newly formed American Association talked him into coming to Cincinnati, and he helped the club take the league's inaugural championship in 1882. He batted only .228 in his rookie season but led the league in putouts, double plays, and fielding average, establishing a pattern of fielding superiority that would last throughout his career.

In all, McPhee led the league at his position in double plays 11 times, fielding average nine times, putouts eight times, and total chances per game and assists six times each. He never led the league in errors. In 1886 he registered an amazing 529 putouts, and in 1893 he became the first player at any position to exceed 100 double plays in a single season. The 529 putouts remain a record, as well as Bid's career total of 6,550 putouts. In addition to setting fielding records, McPhee was instrumental in changing the way the game is played. He was one of the first to play away from the second base bag, and his adroitness at turning two on intentionally dropped pop-ups helped bring about the infield fly rule.

McPhee also gradually improved as a hitter, becoming a tough enough out to serve as the Reds' leadoff batter for several seasons. He scored more than 100 runs in a season 10 different times and hit more triples in the majors through 1892 than any players other than famed sluggers Roger Connor and Dan Brouthers. In addition, McPhee tripled three times in one game off Hall of Famer Amos Rusie and boosted his lifetime batting average to .272 by the time he retired after the 1899 campaign.

Unlike many nineteenth-century ballplayers, McPhee was a gentleman who did not drink, brawl, or carouse, and he was never ejected from a game, a distinction he was proud to claim. On the other hand, his retiring nature did not lend itself to a leadership role among his peers, and his stint as Reds' manager lasted only a season and a half (1901–02).

In retirement McPhee lived in San Diego, from where he once read his premature obituary in *The Sporting News*. Fifty-seven years after his death in 1943, he was finally inducted into the National Baseball Hall of Fame. Although no one accepted the honor on his behalf, a relative present at the Cooperstown ceremony said, "He'd had gnarled fingers but could still write letters in a Spencerian hand."

YEAR	TM	G	AB	R	H	HR	RBI	SB	BB	SO	BA
1882–99	CIN (18 yrs)	2138	8304	1684	2258	53	1072	568	982	377	.272

Edd Roush

Redlegs' center fielder Edd Roush was a tough competitor, a tough out, a tough negotiator, . . . and a tough spell, but Cincinnati fans loved the man whose first and last names both bedeviled sportswriters and typesetters for most of his 18 seasons in major-league baseball.

"Double D," as Roush was called because of the odd spelling of his first name, was born in 1893 on a farm near Oakland City, Indiana, and he grew up performing typical chores, such as rising at four in the morning to milk the family cows. Years later when asked why he'd wanted so desperately to become a professional ballplayer, he said, "Because I had to get away from those damn cows!"

The squeezing of all those udders gave Roush such strong hands and wrists that he was able to control a 48-ounce bat, the heaviest ever used by a major-league player. After a cup of coffee with the Chicago White Sox, Roush established himself as a dangerous batsman in the upstart Federal League, first with Indianapolis and then with Newark. When the Federal League dissolved after two seasons, Roush was sold to the New York Giants. One day after Roush popped up, Giants' manager John McGraw forbade him from using his heavy bat. Roush replied that he was going to keep using the bat and hit .300 with it too. Nobody talked back to McGraw, so halfway through the 1916 season McGraw shipped Roush to Cincinnati. It was the worst trade McGraw ever made, and the Giants' manager spent the next decade trying to get Edd back.

True to his word, the left-handed batting Roush, who choked up and sprayed the ball to all fields, became a perennial .300 hitter. He won National League batting titles for the Reds in 1917 (.341) and 1919

(.321), missed a third title by two points, hit over .300 13 times, and ended his career with a .323 average.

The only time in his life that Roush didn't rake was in the infamous 1919 World Series when White Sox pitchers held him to a .214 average. Despite this uncharacteristic slump, his spectacular fielding made him one of the stars of the Series. He made a number of exciting, rally-snuffing catches, as well as 13 putouts in the first two games alone, prompting one newspaper to gush:

"This series, if nothing else, is stamping Roush as the greatest center-fielder in the game—he has no rivals." Before the final contest of the Series he also read the riot act to his teammates, some of whom were suspected, like the eight dirty "Black Sox" players, of having been paid off by gamblers to do less than their best. To his dying day, the proud Roush insisted that the Reds had been the better team and would have won the Series even if it had been played on the up-and-up.

For most of his career Roush was the Reds' biggest drawing card, and fans came to expect to see him make circus catches at Redland Field, while climbing or wrapping himself around the flagpoles in left- and right-center fields.

As much as Roush loved the game, he detested spring training and became famous as an annual no-show, holding out for more money. He once held out an entire season (1937) and almost always parlayed the threat of not playing into a higher salary. Ironically, in retirement he became a fixture at the Pittsburgh Pirates' spring training complex in Bradenton, Florida, until his death in 1988. He left this world as a Hall of Famer with the added distinction of having been voted by the fans in 1969 as the "Greatest Red Who Ever Lived."

YEAR	TM	G	AB	R	H	HR	RBI	SB	BB	SO	BA
1913	CHW (1 yr)	9	10	2	1	0	0	0	0	2	.100
1914	IND (1 yr)	74	166	26	54	1	30	12	6	20	.325
1915	NEW (1 yr)	145	551	73	164	3	60	28	38	25	.298
1916, 1927–29	NYG (4 yrs)	340	1252	183	373	17	128	29	86	43	.298
1916–26, 1931	CIN (12 yrs)	1399	5384	815	1784	47	763	199	354	170	.331
Total		1967	7363	1099	2376	68	981	268	484	260	.323

Heinie Groh

Heinie Groh is remembered for the fat-barreled, skinny-handled "bottle" bat he used. Old photos often depict him holding the bottle bat in front of his chest, his hands apart, standing in his unorthodox facing-the-pitcher batting stance that is almost as famous as his unusual bat. Neither oddity should obscure the fact that he was a superb ballplayer, the best third baseman of the dead-ball era, and a Cincinnati Reds legend whose credentials make him highly qualified for the National Baseball Hall of Fame.

Born September 18, 1889, in Rochester, New York, Henry Knight Groh certainly did not look or perform like a future major leaguer when he broke into pro ball in 1908 in Oshkosh, Wisconsin. As a five-foot-eight 158-pound short-stop, he ended the season with a batting average just a few points higher than his weight. With his glove as his meal ticket, Groh kept improving as a hitter until he was signed by the New York Giants, who promoted him to the big leagues in 1912. Groh was still so small and youthful-looking that in his first at bat as a pinch hitter, the opposing team, trying to revive the feud between the Giants' manager John McGraw and umpire Bill Klem, almost convinced Klem that McGraw had sent the bat boy up to bat just to embarrass him.

Early in 1913 the Reds acquired Groh in a trade as a throw-in, and "Heinie," as Cincinnati's large German populace took to calling him, quickly became the starting second baseman and leadoff batter. Two years later the Reds installed Groh at the hot corner, where he was equally adept at fielding bunts and knocking down hot smashes with his chest and his glove. He led NL third basemen in double plays seven times, in fielding percent-age five times, and in putouts three times; and in 1924 he set the record for fielding percentage at his position. An excellent bunter and skilled hit-and-run man, Groh also proved he could hit, although he definitely did it his way. Unable to hold the bottle bat down on the knob end and swing from the heels, he spread his smallish hands and chopped at the ball, attempting only to drive it over the heads of the infielders. His method worked pretty well. He batted over .300 four times for the Reds, with a high of .331 in 1921, and crafted a career average of .292. He led the league in hits once and in doubles twice and was regularly among the leaders in walks, doubles, runs, and on-base percentage.

Along with Edd Roush, Groh was the driving force behind the Reds' 1919 World Championship. Like Roush, he always believed the Reds were a better club than the Black Sox and would have triumphed regardless of the Chicago team's intentions. Groh wore out his welcome in Cincinnati by holding out for half of the 1921 season, and he was traded back to McGraw in December for two players and $150,000. It was like throwing Br'er Rabbit into the briar patch, as Groh helped the Giants win three straight NL pennants (1922–24). In helping defeat the Yankees, Groh outshone Babe Ruth by going 9–19 in the 1922 World Series. Heinie relished that achievement by driving around the rest of his life with an auto tag of 474 that referred to his average in that Series. Groh, who still ranks in the Reds' Top 10 for four batting categories, saw most of his records broken but always had a sense of humor about it, claiming he still had one record: "most World Series on the most different teams for a right-handed third baseman who didn't switch-hit and who never played for the Yankees."

YEAR	TM	G	AB	R	H	HR	RBI	SB	BB	SO	BA
1912–13 1922–26	NYG (7 yrs)	451	1600	253	441	9	155	22	181	86	.276
1913–21	CIN (9 yrs)	1211	4439	663	1323	17	408	158	513	257	.298
1927	PIT (1 yr)	14	35	2	10	0	3	0	2	2	.286
Total		1676	6074	918	1774	26	566	180	696	345	.292

Dummy Hoy

When William Ellsworth Hoy was three years old, he contracted spinal meningitis and became deaf. He grew up not only to lead a normal, productive life but also to enjoy the greatest baseball career of any seriously handicapped player. Hoy's happiest days in the big leagues were spent with the Cincinnati Reds, and the Queen City has always been proud to claim this courageous ballplayer as one of her favorite adopted sons.

Born in Houcktown, Ohio, near Findlay on May 23, 1862, Hoy breezed through the Ohio State School for the Deaf in Columbus and graduated as valedictorian. He operated a small shoe repair shop in his hometown and played weekend ball until he was able to hook on with Oshkosh of the Northwestern League in 1886. His fine play in '87 resulted in his being signed by Washington of the National League.

Although Washington was a terrible team in 1888, Hoy had a splendid rookie season, batting .274, leading the league in stolen bases (82), and setting rookie records for games, at bats, hits, singles, and walks. No bigger than five feet six and 160 pounds, the left-handed hitting Hoy didn't have much power, but he was extremely fast and had a good eye. Throughout his career he walked a lot, and he scored 100-plus runs nine times. He was also an excellent center fielder who played very shallow. On June 19, 1889, he threw out three runners at home plate in one game for Washington.

Hoy played for another bad team in 1890, Buffalo of the short-lived Players League, and then finally caught on with a winner, the St. Louis Browns of the American Association. Dummy scored 136 runs and led the league in walks (117) for the 1891 champion Browns who let him go after the season rather than meet his salary demands.

After the merger of the AA with the National League, Hoy wound up back in Washington for two more seasons. In November 1893 Washington made a mistake, trading Hoy to Cincinnati for a mediocre pitcher. In the next four years Hoy batted .304, .277, .298, and .292 and enjoyed his status as one of the most popular players on the Reds.

While recent historians have doubted that umpire hand signals originated with a request by Hoy, they acknowledge that his enthusiasm for such gestures helped solidify their use as routine. Similarly, some believe that Hoy's reputed muteness was not total. In 1900 *The Sporting News* claimed that Hoy made utterances in a high, squeaky voice, while earlier the paper reported that the outfielder could call something akin to "I'll take it" for fly balls. As for Hoy's nickname, it would be a mistake to assume that it was created out of malice. Ball fans, especially in Cincinnati, respected Hoy, and crowds would stand en masse to wave their arms and hats to acknowledge a good play on his part. And Hoy himself liked the nickname, even requesting that it continue to appear in one newspaper that had discontinued its use.

Hoy had two good years in Louisville of the National League, hitting over .300 both seasons, and played on another pennant winner for Chicago in 1901, during the American League's inaugural year. His stint with the White Stockings gave Dummy the distinction of being one of 29 players to play in four different major leagues. Hoy ended his career with 2,048 hits and 1,429 runs (81st all time). He married a deaf teacher of the deaf, and one of their three children became a judge in Cincinnati. As the oldest living former major leaguer at the time, Dummy threw out the first ball of Game 3 in the 1961 World Series and died that December at age 99.

YEAR	TM	G	AB	R	H	HR	RBI	SB	BB	SO	BA
1888–89 1892–93	WAS (4 yrs)	545	2167	389	582	5	188	225	296	10	.268
1890	BUF (1 yr)	122	493	107	147	1	53	39	94	36	.298
1891	STL (1 yr)	139	559	134	163	5	64	59	117	25	.292
1894–97, 1902	CIN (5 yrs)	556	2151	466	630	16	245	176	302	87	.293
1898–99	LOU (2 yrs)	303	1218	221	371	11	115	70	111	64	.305
1901	CHW (1 yr)	132	527	112	155	2	60	27	86	23	.294
Total		1797	7115	1429	2048	40	725	596	1006	245	.288

Noodles Hahn

He had ambition, a good head on his shoulders, and a fastball he used like a buzz saw. He was an accomplished star, the first great Reds' pitcher of the twentieth century, at an age when most young players struggled to establish themselves as big leaguers. And then suddenly it was over. Noodles Hahn was out of baseball, not the victim of the opponents' ability to hit him but the victim of his own insatiable desire to toe the rubber.

Frank George Hahn was born April 29, 1879, in Nashville, Tennessee. He claimed not to know where his catchy nickname came from, but it certainly had something to do with his mother's homemade soup: either his own taste for it or, as one friend averred, the fact that as a boy Frank was required to carry it to his father's workplace at lunchtime.

In any case, Noodles had a left arm bestowed on him by the gods. In 1895 as an amateur 16-year-old, he shut out the Nashville club of the Southern League, who signed him and took him along when the franchise shifted to Mobile. He pitched well enough the next year to move up to Detroit in the Western League, where, despite having a losing record, he impressed St. Paul owner Charles Comiskey who recommended him to the Reds. From the Reds' spring training camp of 1899, *The Sporting News* reported that Hahn had "terrific speed, good curves, and the best control ever displayed by a green southpaw." Reds' manager Buck Ewing supposedly did not want to take the kid north; owner John Brush insisted that he did.

Noodles justified Brush's faith in him and then some. The rookie went 23–8 with an ERA of 2.68 and led the National League in strikeouts with 145. Hahn showed early what he was made of during a 1–0 May 11 shutout of the Pirates in Pittsburgh. After giving up a leadoff triple in the ninth, Noodles set the baseball on the ground, as if he were conceding defeat. The delay was merely a chance for him to stuff some tobacco in his mouth, after which he picked up the ball and proceeded to strike out the side. Pittsburgh manager Patsy Donovan later called the performance "the greatest game I ever saw a young pitcher deliver."

Many a ballplayer of the era drank his career to a premature end. Not Noodles, who proclaimed after the season, "This year shows me what I can do when I'm not drinking. I'll never again indulge in any kind of strong drink." The next year Hahn pitched the century's first no-hitter against a Philadelphia contingent that was the best-hitting team in the league.

While Hahn did not surrender to demon rum, he was unable to apply the same temperance to his pitching. In his six full seasons with Cincinnati, he averaged 317 innings pitched. In 1901, when he won 22 games, led the league in strikeouts for the third straight year, and completed 41 of the 42 games he started, he reeled off a yeomanly 375 IP. Hahn knew the danger he was flirting with, admitting, "I am wise enough to know that I cannot last forever and that I am greatly shortening my career by pitching as I did last season."

Indeed he did. "The Great Hahn," as the press had begun to call him, won 23 games in 1902 and 22 in '03; but after a 16–18 slate in 1904 he lost his fastball and won only eight more major league games. Noodles, who'd earned a degree in veterinary science, became a government meat inspector in Cincinnati. To no one's surprise, he pitched batting practice for the Reds as late as 1946, when he was 67 years old.

Year	Tm	W	L	ERA	GS	CG	SHO	IP	H	R	BB	SO
1899–05	CIN (7 yrs)	127	92	2.52	225	209	24	1987.1	1878	799	375	900
1906	NYG (1 YR)	3	2	3.86	6	3	1	42	38	22	6	17
Total		130	94	2.55	231	212	25	2029.1	1916	821	381	917

Bubbles Hargrave

Catchers seldom hit for high average because of their legs. Slow-footed players often wind up behind the plate to start with because they don't have to cover the ground other players do, and whatever speed a catcher begins with is reduced by the constant strain the job puts on his legs. Modern National League batting titles have been captured by only two catchers, and both of them played for the Cincinnati Reds: Ernie Lombardi and a sturdy Hoosier fireplug named Bubbles Hargrave.

Born July 15, 1892, in New Haven, Indiana, Eugene Franklin Hargrave was a stutterer, who had difficulty pronouncing the letter *b*. He detested the resulting nickname of Bubbles because its flighty connotation did not mesh with his vocation and self-image as a tough, no-nonsense backstop.

Hargrave began his pro career as a 19-year-old in 1911 with Terre Haute, Indiana, and wasn't able to win a job as a regular in the majors until he was 28. The Chicago Cubs signed him in 1913, but in three years with them he appeared in only 41 games. The undiscouraged Hargrave made little progress up the minor league ladder until he hooked on with St. Paul of the American Association in 1919. The Reds bought him after he hit .335 the next year.

Seasoned by his long apprenticeship in the bushes, Bubbles was ready for the big time and the responsibilities of handling what was for most of the rest of the decade the best pitching staff in the National League. He batted .289 in his rookie year of 1921 and over .300 for the next six years.

Despite his poise and strong arm, which held down the running game of the Reds' opponents, the right-handed hitting Hargrave platooned his entire eight-year Reds' career. From 1921 through 1925 he shared the catching duties with left-handed batting Ivy Wingo, who held the major-league record for games played by a catcher when he retired, and from 1926 through 1928 with Val Picinich.

The most games Hargrave played in one season was 118 in 1923, when he enjoyed his best overall year. He hit .333 with career highs in home runs (10) and RBI (78). In 1926, when Hargrave won the NL batting crown, he appeared in 105 games, an important total since at the time 100 games played was the minimum qualification for the title. In batting a robust .353, Bubbles had 115 hits in 326 at bats and 365 plate appearances, 137 PA short of the 502 that are required today. Hargrave ended Rogers Hornsby's run of six straight batting titles and became the first catcher in the NL to cop a batting title since King Kelly of the 1886 White Stockings.

When asked what had happened to make him the leading hitter in the league, Hargrave said, "It was because I was sick in the spring." What Hargrave was referring to was a bout of appendicitis. Doctors wanted to operate when the attack hit, but Bubbles refused to go under the knife. Instead he went on a strict diet and for a time ate no solid foods at all, relying on gallons of buttermilk, which he had liberally drunk while growing up in Indiana. He lost 14 pounds, and the diet even seemed to improve his vision. Hargrave was certainly the first batting champ to be fortified with drink as mild as buttermilk.

Had the All-Star Game been invented, Hargrave would have made the NL squad several times. He was, in fact, one of four Reds named by baseball writers to an honorary NL All-Star team after the 1925 season. After retiring from baseball, he lived in Cincinnati where he was a supervisor at a valve company.

YEAR	TM	G	AB	R	H	HR	RBI	SB	BB	SO	BA
1913–15	CHC (3 yrs)	41	58	5	12	0	5	2	1	9	.207
1921–28	CIN (8 yrs)	766	2367	298	744	29	359	27	206	147	.314
1930	NYY (1 yr)	45	108	11	30	0	12	0	10	9	.278
Total		852	2533	314	786	29	376	29	217	165	.310

Eppa Rixey

The talented Tom Seaver brought his powerful right arm to Cincinnati halfway through his career. He performed brilliantly but didn't stay long, leaving Reds' fans to wish he'd come earlier and stayed later. Five decades earlier another pretty fair pitcher came to Cincinnati in mid-career, but unlike Seaver he found a home in the Queen City, where he prospered and became the winningest hurler in team history.

Eppa Rixey Jr., a lanky six-foot-five left-handed pitcher came to the National League in 1912 straight out of the University of Virginia. His coach there, Cy Rigler, who helped develop him into an effective hurler, also happened to be a scout for the Philadelphia Phillies, as well as an NL umpire. Rixey was promised a $2,000 bonus to sign but never got it, which caused a rift for a while between him and Rigler; until Rixey learned that his coach had always assumed that the Phillies had made good on their promise.

In 1916 under the tutelage of Phillies' manager Pat Moran, Rixey blossomed into a 22-game winner with an ERA of 1.85. Rixey wasn't as successful the next three years. He had a losing record each summer and twice lost more than 20 games. Meanwhile, Moran's vaunted pitching staff, which had won the 1919 NL pennant in Pat's first year at the helm in Cincinnati, suddenly disintegrated, making Garry Hermann amenable to a trade with Philadelphia and reuniting Moran with his pet project, "The Eiffel Tower of Culpeper, Virginia."

Rixey, pushing 30 when the Reds acquired him, immediately justified Moran's faith in him. He won 19 games in 1921 and the next year chalked up a league-high 25 victories against 13 defeats. He was a 20-game winner again in 1923—the last time a Reds' left-hander won 20 until Jim Merritt did it in 1970—along with Dolf Luque (who won 27 games) and Pete Donohue (who copped another 21). The trio of Rixey, Luque, and Donohue became the Reds' "Big Three" and formed the core of what functioned for the next decade as the best pitching staff in the National League. No other National League team has featured three 20-game winners in the same season since the Reds in '23.

Although sportswriter Lee Allen opined that Rixey represented the maximum height a player might attain without sacrificing coordination and grace, Rixey was not a hard thrower. He was, on the contrary, a nibbler and a teaser, who got by on his smarts and by adroitly changing speeds. The holder of a master's degree in chemistry from the University of Virginia, Rixey was often behind the hitters but used those counts to his advantage. "The hitters always look for the fastball when they get ahead and are always shocked when they don't get it," he said. A workhorse because of his arm-saving approach, Rixey pitched more than 300 innings three years in a row. He seldom gave up the long ball either. In 1921 he was touched for one home run in 301 innings.

A hard loser who wrecked many a clubhouse after a tough loss, Rixey was nevertheless a gentleman away from the diamond, known for "his courtly manner and pleasant drawl," according to Allen. A modest man, he was unaware until informed by sportswriter Tom Swope that he retired as the winningest left-handed pitcher in National League history. Not until Warren Spahn won his 267th game a quarter of a century later did he relinquish that title. To this day he remains the Reds' career leader in starts (356), innings pitched (2,890), and victories (179). He was elected to the Reds' Hall of Fame in 1959 and to the National Baseball Hall of Fame in 1963.

Year	Tm	W	L	ERA	GS	CG	SHO	IP	H	R	BB	SO
1912–20	PHP (8 yrs)	87	103	2.83	197	110	14	1604	1518	682	479	690
1921–33	CIN (13 yrs)	179	148	3.33	357	180	23	2890.2	3115	1304	603	660
Total		266	251	3.15	554	290	37	4494.2	4633	1986	1082	1350

Cy Seymour

Cy Seymour is hardly the only major leaguer to have been a pitcher before he became a position player; however, no modern player other than Seymour and Babe Ruth has ever led a league in a major pitching category, pitched 100 games, and batted more than 1,500 times. While Seymour, named after Cy Young, did not make anybody forget about Ruth, he did become the Reds' first great hitter of the twentieth century, setting records that remain team standards more than a century later.

James Bentley Seymour was born December 9, 1872, in Albany, New York. He became known to the wider world as a pitcher for a semipro outfit in Plattsburgh, New York, where he was paid so well that he was unwilling to leave until beckoned by the New York Giants. His hot temper and lack of control caused him to get bounced back and forth to the minors and resulted in a lackluster 2–4 record and 6.40 ERA for New York in 1896. Although he led the National League in walks the next three years, he did win 18 games in 1897 and 25 more in 1898 after developing an "indrop" pitch, known today as a screwball. It was in 1898 that he led the NL in strikeouts with 239 (26 more than he walked).

Just when he seemed to be getting it together as a pitcher, the left-handed throwing and batting Seymour started having arm problems in 1899, due partly to his use of the indrop. His record slid to 14–18, and once again he walked more batters than he whiffed. His .327 average in 159 at bats caused him to start seriously considering making the switch from pitching to hitting.

Things came to a head in 1900. Seymour held out for higher pay, developed a sore arm, and had trouble getting along with Giants' manager Buck Ewing and his replacement, George Davis. Twice suspended without pay, he worked only 31 innings while recording an ERA of 6.96.

Fortunately for Seymour, John McGraw came to the rescue, making Cy the right fielder of his 1901 Baltimore American League entry. Seymour celebrated the start of the second stage of his career by batting .303 in 134 games. When McGraw broke up the team halfway through the next season, Seymour bolted for Cincinnati, where he began his great run with the Reds. In his first three and a half seasons, he batted .340, .342, .313, and, in 1905, .377, which was an astounding 122 points above the league average. In addition to winning the batting title in 1905, Seymour led the league in hits, doubles, triples, RBI, slugging percentage, and total bases. The only thing that kept him from winning the NL Triple Crown was the home run hit by the Reds' Fred Odwell on the last day of the season, which broke a tie in homers between the two teammates.

Seymour had an unusual batting style. He batted off his front foot and, unlike most hitters of the day, hit from the back of the batter's box. He was a contact, place hitter who constantly used the run and hit play to find holes vacated by fielders covering the bases against his teammates on the move. He also changed bats frequently, counterintuitively using light bats against slower pitchers and heavy bats against faster ones.

Seymour was batting .257 when the Reds sold him back to the Giants in mid-1906 for $12,000, the highest price yet paid for a ballplayer. After the Giants cut him loose in 1910, he retired with a lifetime average of .303. He died nine years later from tuberculosis, carrying into eternity what remain as the Reds' single-season highest batting average and career average of .332.

YEAR	TM	G	AB	R	H	HR	RBI	SB	BB	SO	BA
1896–00 1906–10	NYG (10 yrs)	728	2565	300	732	22	345	96	152	173	.285
1901–02	BAL (2 yrs)	206	827	122	241	4	118	50	46	48	.291
1902–06	CIN (5 yrs)	556	2221	313	738	26	326	74	149	133	.332
1913	BOS (1 yr)	39	73	2	13	0	10	2	7	7	.178
Total		1529	5686	737	1724	52	799	222	354	361	.303

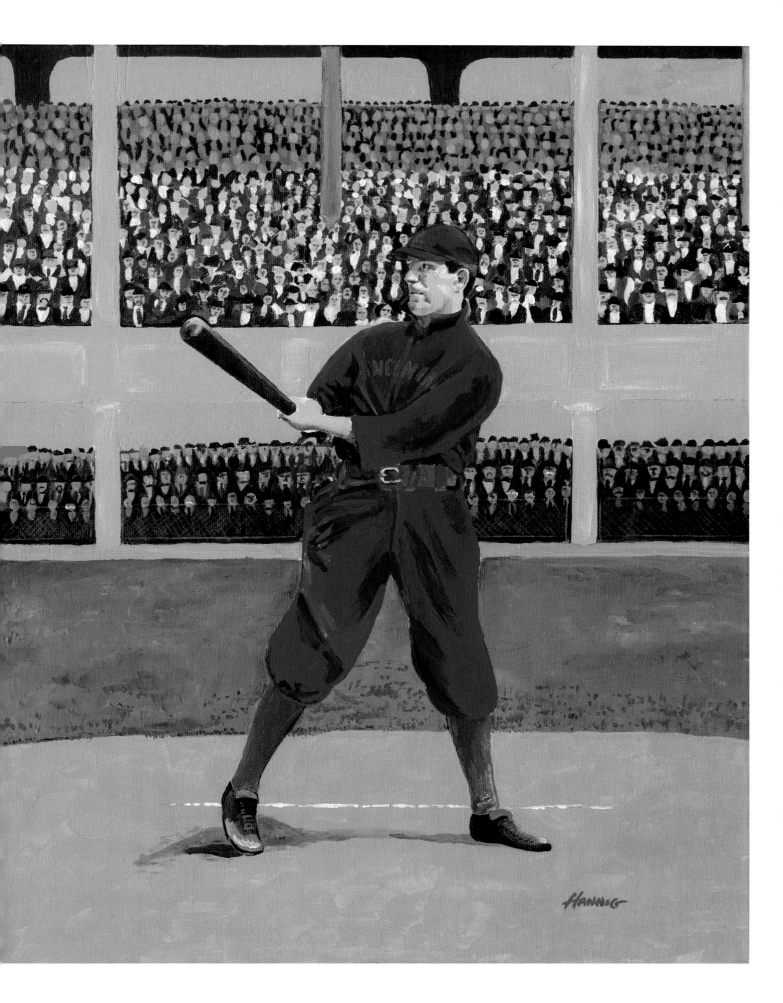

1926–1950

Dolph Luque

Long before Reds' fans adored Tony Perez . . . long before Perez was even born . . . Reds' rooters had another Cuban player to cheer for, a stocky, no-nonsense pitcher named Adolfo Domingo de Guzman Luque. Known as "The Pride of Havana," Luque not only broke barriers and gained respect for his fellow Hispanics, he also achieved the greatest single season record of any pitcher in team history.

Luque was brought to the United States by Dr. Hernandez Henriquez to play for his Long Branch, New Jersey, team of the New York–New Jersey League. Luque's 22–5 record for Long Branch in 1913 caught the eye of the Boston Braves, who signed him late in 1914. Luque failed to stick with Boston, but his solid work for the Louisville Colonels at the start of the 1918 season prompted the Reds to buy him and give him 10 starts that summer. Luque was allowed to play in the National League because he was not as dark-skinned as his countrymen, such as Hall of Fame pitcher Martin Dihigo. The next year Luque went 9–3, mostly out of the bullpen, to help the Reds win their first National League pennant and then pitched five scoreless innings in two games of the 1919 World Series.

In 1920 Luque was worked into the starting rotation and posted a 13–9 record, beginning a streak of nine consecutive seasons in which he won 10 or more games for Cincinnati. Despite good ERAs, Dolph had losing records in 1921 and '22. That changed big-time in 1923, when he became the National League King of the Hill. With his 27–8 record, he led the league in wins and winning percentage, and his ERA of 1.93 was a whopping .84 points lower than his closest rival. His 151 strikeouts, the second-highest total in the league, were easily enough to give him the team's pitching Triple Crown. Pete Donohue won 21 games and Eppa Rixey 20; yet the 1923 club, the

only one in Reds' history to have three 20-game winners, still finished second to the New York Giants.

Luque had a good fastball, a wicked curve, and a somewhat mean disposition that helped him command the inside corner of the plate and handle out-of-line adversaries when necessary. In one infamous incident at Redland Field, Luque charged into the Giants' dugout and tried to punch Bill Cunningham, a reserve outfielder, who'd been mercilessly heckling him. When Cunningham ducked, Luque's wild swing landed upside the head of the innocent Casey Stengel. A riot ensued and led to the infuriated pitcher's ejection.

For the rest of his Reds' career, Luque suffered from poor offensive support. Never a big winner again, he had a losing record (16–18) even in 1925 when he led the league in ERA (2.63) for the second time. When he was traded to Brooklyn before the 1930 season, he left Cincinnati with a 154–152 record and an ERA of 3.09. His win total is the fourth highest in team history behind only Rixey, Paul Derringer, and Bucky Walters.

After two years in Brooklyn, Luque was released and then signed by the Giants for whom he pitched the final four seasons of his career, mostly in relief. "Papa," as the 42-year-old Luque was then called, won eight games in relief and saved four others to help the Giants win the 1933 pennant. He then nailed down the Giants' World Series conquest of the Washington Senators, hurling 4⅓ innings of shutout ball in the fifth and final game.

Luque won 93 games in the Cuban winter leagues as a pitcher and 565 as a manager over 24 campaigns. A legend of Cincinnati and Havana baseball, he was eulogized upon his death in 1957 for his "fearless heart" by famous sportswriter Frank Graham.

Year	Tm	W	L	ERA	GS	CG	SHO	IP	H	R	BB	SO
1914–15	BSN (2 yr)	0	1	3.95	2	1	0	13.2	11	8	8	4
1918–29	CIN (12 yrs)	154	152	3.09	321	183	24	2668.2	2619	1138	756	970
1930–31	BRO (2 yrs)	21	14	4.39	39	21	2	301.2	343	166	85	87
1932–35	NYG (4 yrs)	19	12	3.47	5	1	0	236.1	258	100	69	69
Total		194	179	3.24	367	206	26	3220.1	3231	1412	918	1130

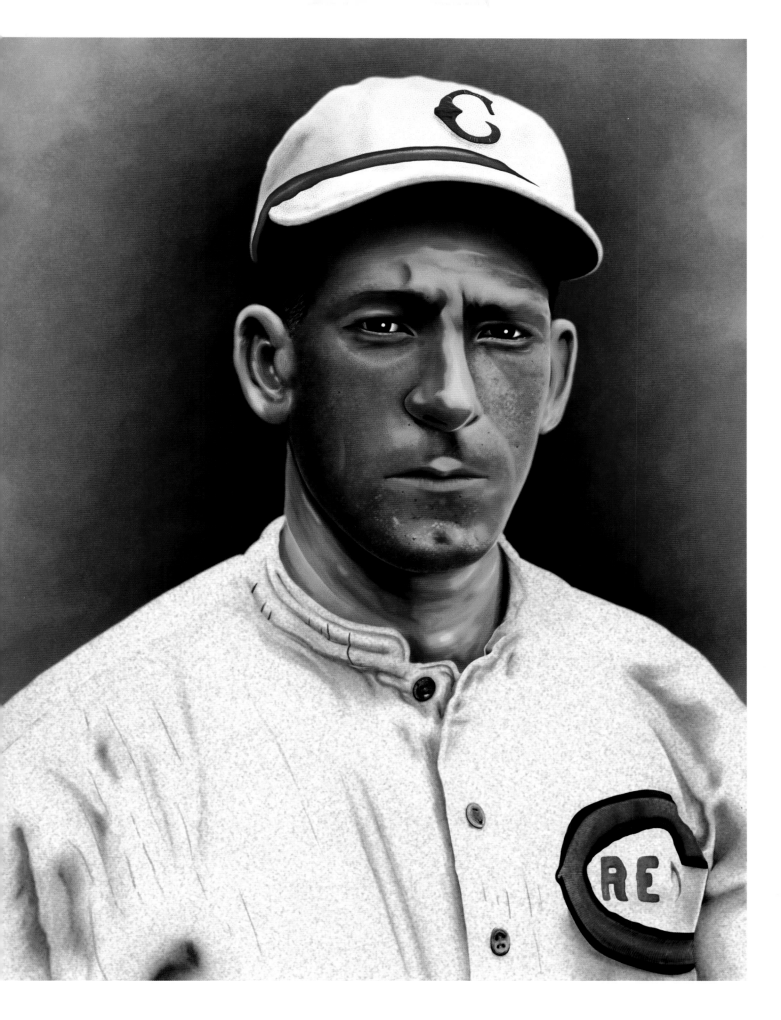

Ernie Lombardi

No player in Reds' history ever epitomized both colorfulness and misfortune more than Ernie Lombardi, a catcher famous for his slowness afoot and a bat that scorched infields and ripped off National League fielders' gloves for 17 years. Infielders retreated in trepidation against Lombardi and often were still able to throw him out from deep in the grass. Nevertheless, the big catcher, who could palm seven baseballs in one hand and used an interlocking grip to swing the heaviest bat in the league, batted over .300 10 times and finished his career with a lifetime average of .306. Kidded unceasingly about his big nose and lack of speed, the shy "Schnozz" took it all in stride, even joking at his own expense. "Pee Wee Reese [Brooklyn shortstop] was in the league three years before I realized he wasn't an outfielder," he once quipped. Female Reds' fans especially loved him, and he became, in the words of Lee Allen, "the most popular player in the history of the club, even more of a hero than Edd Roush had been." Unfortunately, that adulation and his accomplishments never won him the recognition he would later in life crave so desperately.

After his rookie year with the Dodgers, Lombardi came to Cincinnati in 1932 in one of the best trades the Reds ever made. He immediately improved a team that had been foundering in the second division for years, and beginning in '35 he batted .343, .333, .334, and .342. For becoming only the second catcher to win a major league batting title, he earned the NL MVP Award in 1938, which was also the year he caught Johnny Vander Meer's back-to-back no-hitters. The following year, of course, the Reds won their first pennant in two decades and then met the dynastic Yankees in a Fall Classic, which was entirely forgettable, save for one unusual play involving Lombardi.

In the 10th inning of Game 4, Joe DiMaggio lined a single into right field that scored Frank Crosetti easily from third and Charlie Keller from first after Ival Goodman fumbled the ball. As Keller crossed the plate, he collided with Lombardi, who then lay sprawled and dazed in the dirt as the alert DiMaggio sped around the bases and slid across home with the final run of the Yanks' 7–4 victory. New York's sweep of the Series hardly hinged on the play, nor did Game 4, for that matter, yet the press had a field day criticizing Ernie for what became known as "Lombardi's Snooze." For the rest of his life, that stigma burdened the modest Lombardi, who never explained that Keller had accidentally kicked him in the groin.

After batting .319 to help the Reds win another pennant in 1940, Lombardi felt he deserved a raise. General manager Warren Giles thought differently. At a banquet after the Reds' defeat of the Detroit Tigers in the World Series, a tipsy Lombardi at the speaker's podium called Giles "a cheap old goat." Giles took serious offense to the remark, never forgave it, and traded Lombardi to the lowly Boston Braves after the 1941 season. All Ernie did was win his second NL batting title with an average of .330.

Unable to find suitable employment in baseball after his playing days, Lombardi began to resent having been scapegoated, and his brooding led to a near-fatal suicide attempt in 1953. The vengeful Giles, a fixture on the Veterans Committee, was able to keep the increasingly embittered Lombardi, who died in 1977, from ever smelling the roses of Cooperstown. The electors finally gave him the nod in '86, 28 years after he had been made a member of the Reds' inaugural Hall of Fame class.

YEAR	TM	G	AB	R	H	HR	RBI	SB	BB	SO	BA
1931	BRO (1 yr)	73	182	20	54	4	23	1	12	12	.297
1932–41	CIN (10 yrs)	1203	3980	420	1238	120	682	5	264	158	.311
1942	BSN (1 yr)	105	309	32	102	11	46	1	37	12	.330
1943–47	NYG (5 yrs)	472	1384	129	398	55	239	1	117	80	.288
Total		1853	5855	601	1792	190	990	8	430	262	.306

Bucky Walters

In June 1938 Reds' fans were beside themselves with excitement over the pitching exploits of "Double No-hit" Johnny Vander Meer. Had they been able to foresee the future, they would have been happier about Cincinnati's acquisition of another pitcher—despite his losing record—who arrived in the midst of the hoopla over Vandy's fabulous feat. William Henry Walters may have come to Ohio unheralded, but he transformed overnight into the best pitcher in baseball and a Cincinnati baseball legend.

Bucky Walters, born April 19, 1909, was signed off the sandlots of his hometown Philadelphia and started his professional baseball career with Montgomery, Alabama, of the Class B Southeastern League in 1930. Originally a pitcher, he quickly washed out as a moundsman and switched to the hot corner because he was a good hitter. The Boston Braves rescued him, but in two partial seasons with them he hit .211 and .187, earning a demotion back to the minors. His .376 batting clip in 91 games for the San Francisco Missions convinced the Boston Red Sox to give him a try, but by early 1934 the Sox had given up on him too and traded him to the Phillies. It was in Philadelphia that Walters encountered the man who would change his life, player-manager Jimmie Wilson, a veteran catcher.

Cognizant of Walters's strong arm, Wilson urged Bucky to try pitching again. Wilson was so certain the reluctant right-hander could pitch that he even promised him a cash bonus for every game he won. To make Wilson happy, Walters threw a couple of games at the end of the 1934 season and then made the switch for good in 1935 when it became obvious that Johnny Vergez was destined to hold the job as the Phillies' regular third

baseman. Walters progressed slowly. He lost 21 games in 1936, never got his ERA for the woeful Phillies under 4, and carried a 38–53 record with him when Philadelphia sent him to Cincinnati halfway through the 1938 season.

Finally working for a good team and benefiting from the lessons he'd learned the hard way, Walters looked like a new pitcher. He went 11–6 in his first half season with the Reds, and the next year in 1939 he turned in a simply brilliant performance. He captured the National League's pitching Triple Crown, leading the league in wins (27), ERA (2.29), and strikeouts (137) and won the MVP Award for leading the Reds to the pennant. He led the league in wins (22) and ERA (2.48) again the next year, as he and best friend Paul Derringer formed the top pitching combo in the majors. Walters had a third 20-win season in 1944 and also came up big in two of the most important games in Reds' history, defeating the Tigers in Game Two of the 1940 World Series after the Reds had lost five straight Fall Classic contests and evening the same Series by winning Game 6.

Relying on a sinking fastball, a sweeping curve, and excellent control, Walters chalked up the most wins (121) between 1939 and 1944 of any major-league pitcher while posting the lowest ERA (2.67, minimum 1,000 IP). A six-time All-Star, he won 10 or more games for Cincinnati in nine straight seasons and fashioned an ERA under 3 seven times. He was also an excellent fielder and a dangerous hitter, 11 of his 23 home runs coming after he switched to pitching. He finished two wins shy of 200, and his 160 victories as a Red ranks third in team history. His brief unsuccessful stint as Reds' manager did not tarnish his star in the least; his brilliance on the mound continues to shine in the annals of Reds' history.

Year	Tm	W	L	ERA	GS	CG	SHO	IP	H	R	BB	SO
1934–38	PHP (5 yrs)	38	53	4.48	102	47	10	745	843	436	313	228
1938–48	CIN (11 yrs)	160	107	2.93	296	195	32	2355.2	2142	905	806	879
1950	BSN (1 yr)	0	0	4.50	0	0	0	4	5	2	2	0
Total		198	160	3.30	398	242	42	3104.2	2990	1343	1121	1107

Paul Derringer

Would you trade a troublesome "good field–no hit" shortstop for a big stud capable of becoming the ace of your pitching staff? You sure would, and that's what the Reds did on May 7, 1933. They packed Leo Durocher off to the St. Louis Cardinals for right-handed Samuel Paul Derringer, who would become one of the best pitchers in Cincinnati history, while leading the team to its first World Championship in two decades.

The son of a tobacco farmer in Springfield, Kentucky, Derringer was discovered by the Cardinals in 1926 while pitching for a mining team in Coalwood, West Virginia. It took Derringer four years to climb out of the Cardinals' deep farm system, but after he won a combined 40 games to lead Rochester to consecutive International League pennants, he was ready for the majors. He was so impressive in the spring of 1931 that Branch Rickey chose him for the big league roster over Dizzy Dean. His 18–8 record as a rookie led the NL in winning percentage, while the 33 consecutive scoreless innings he hurled in September inspired manager Gabby Street to start him in the first game of the World Series. The Philadelphia A's battered him in that game and in Game 4 too, causing Derringer to lose some confidence in his abilities. An off year in 1932 and a slow start in 1933, plus the Cards' need for a shortstop, prompted the trade that paid huge dividends to the Reds.

Derringer lost 25 games for the Reds in 1933 but still earned a raise of $1,500. After all, his ERA was 3.23 and the Reds were a terrible team, who were shut out in seven of Derringer's losses. In 1935 when he won 22 games, he was the only Reds' pitcher to win in double figures. As the Reds slowly improved, Derringer became the rock upon which the championship team's foundation was built. With the acquisition of Bucky Walters

from Philadelphia, Cincinnati suddenly boasted the best one-two punch in baseball. For the pennant-winning club in 1939, Derringer posted a career-best record of 25–7, and he followed that with a 20–12 mark for the 1940 champs, his fourth and final 20-win season.

Derringer was famous for one of the most exaggerated skyscraping leg kicks ever used by a big league pitcher, yet his control was superb. In 3,646 innings pitched, he walked 761 batters for a walk ratio of 1.88, the third lowest in NL history at the time. In 301 innings of work in 1939, he gave away only 35 free passes, and 12 of those were intentional.

Because of Derringer's bearlike physique and short temper, the fans called the big pitcher "Oom Paul." The players referred to him as "Duke" because he was such a fancy dresser, known to change clothes as many as five times a day. Although he lost the first four World Series games he pitched, Derringer was considered a clutch performer. Despite giving up 14 hits, he defeated the Cardinals 5–3 in the pennant-clinching game of 1939, and he beat the Tigers 2–1 on two days' rest to win Game 7 and secure the 1940 World Championship for the Reds.

After that triumph, Derringer seemed to lose his touch, and the Reds sold him to Chicago in 1943. His final productive season came when he won 16 games to help the Cubs cop the 1945 pennant. He ended his 15-year career with a 223–212 record, 32 shutouts, and six All-Star Game selections (including two starts). His 161 wins in a Reds' uniform were good for third place. Derringer had his run-ins with teammates and management, but the fans were always behind him and put him in the team's first Hall of Fame class.

Year	Tm	W	L	ERA	GS	CG	SHO	IP	H	R	BB	SO
1931–33	STL (3 yrs)	29	24	3.74	55	30	5	462	545	232	141	215
1933–42	CIN (10yrs)	161	150	3.36	322	189	24	2615.1	2755	1135	491	1062
1943–45	CHC (3 yrs)	33	38	3.71	68	32	3	567.2	612	285	129	230
Total		223	212	3.46	445	251	32	3645	3912	1652	761	1507

Frank McCormick

No Reds' player ever had a more spectacular debut than Frank Andrew McCormick, the big first baseman whose lusty hitting in the first three years of his career catapulted Cincinnati to back-to-back NL pennants and the World Championship of 1940. Without McCormick, the champagne at Crosley would never have been uncorked. The Reds might have enjoyed more bubbly, and sooner, had they not let McCormick languish in the minors as long as they did.

Born June 9, 1911, in Manhasset, New York, the handsome McCormick grew up in the same Manhattan neighborhood as Lou Gehrig, who naturally became his idol. After unsuccessful tryouts with three other major league teams as an outfielder, McCormick borrowed $50 from an uncle to travel to Beckley, West Virginia, to work out as a first baseman for the Reds' affiliate there. Beckley took a chance on him, and he hit so well for the Middle Atlantic League entry in 1934 that he earned a September look-see in Cincinnati, during which he batted .313 in 12 games. Asked if he could hit Brooklyn hurler Emil Leonard, the nervous but game McCormick said, "I can hit any pitcher." Indeed he could, but it took a few more years to convince the Reds.

In 1936 McCormick hit .381 for Durham and led the league in every meaningful batting category. While batting .322 in the International League in 1937, McCormick bounced between Syracuse and Cincinnati. He finally earned a permanent spot on the Reds' roster after cracking seven hits in a September doubleheader.

As if he were making a "what took you so long" statement to the Reds, Frank tore up the NL as a 26-year-old rookie in 1938 and in the next two seasons as well. He batted .327, .332, and .309; knocked in 106, 128, and 127

runs; hit 40 or more doubles each year; and became only the third player in history (along with Rogers Hornsby and Ginger Beaumont) to lead the league in hits three consecutive years. For his crucial contributions to the Reds' offense, he was named the NL MVP in 1940.

Unable to maintain that level of superiority due to a back injury he suffered in 1940, McCormick remained a big bat in the Reds' lineup for years and wound up leading the team in batting average six consecutive seasons, in hits six times, in doubles seven times, in home runs four times, and in RBI seven times. He was an NL All-Star seven times.

A notorious first-pitch fastball hitter, McCormick once explained his approach at the plate, saying, "I learned early that pitchers try to sneak a good one by you to get ahead in the count. I didn't let it go by." Nevertheless, he was difficult to strike out. In 5,723 at bats, he whiffed only 189 times for a ratio of 1:30. A good fielder, he led NL first basemen in fielding percentage four times and put together an errorless streak of 1,325 chances. Along with Lonnie Frey, Billy Myers, and Bill Werber, he was a member of the Reds' "Jungle Club" infield of 1939–40 and went by the nickname "Wildcat."

After finishing up with the Phillies and Red Sox, McCormick managed in the minors for several years, winning a Canadian-American League pennant and championship with Quebec in 1949. He later scouted and coached for the Reds, broadcast Reds' games from 1958 to the mid-1960s, and ran the New York Yankees' ticket operations until his death in 1982. In 1958 he was inducted into the Reds Hall of Fame as a member of the inaugural class, along with former teammates Paul Derringer, Ernie Lombardi, Johnny Vander Meer, and Bucky Walters.

YEAR	TM	G	AB	R	H	HR	RBI	SB	BB	SO	BA
1934 1937–45	CIN (10 yrs)	1228	4787	631	1439	110	803	23	339	149	.301
1946–47	PHP (2 yrs)	150	544	53	152	12	74	2	39	23	.279
1947–48	BSN (2 yrs)	156	392	38	120	6	77	2	21	17	.306
Total		1534	5723	722	1711	128	954	27	399	189	.299

Ival Goodman

Right fielder Ival Goodman got a late start as a major leaguer but made the most of his opportunity and today is remembered as a key component of the Reds' championship teams of 1939 and '40. Born in 1908 in Northview, Missouri, Goodman was signed by the St. Louis Cardinals, who farmed him out to Washington Senators' minor-league clubs for three seasons, after which he started his climb through the Cardinals' system. His stellar year with Rochester of the International League convinced the Cardinals that he was ready for the big leagues, but they had no room for him and so sold him to the Reds for $20,000 at the 1934 winter meetings. That was the break needed by Goodman, who made his major league debut in 1935 as a 26-year-old.

Goodman solidified the Reds' outfield with good speed, fine glove work, and a strong throwing arm; while at bat he provided some sorely needed power. As a rookie playing in cavernous Crosley Field, he led the NL in triples with 18 and, with 322, broke Babe Ruth's record for putouts as a rookie right fielder. He hit the most triples in the league again the following year, led the Reds in slugging percentage five straight years, and after the team finally adjusted its ballpark to more human dimensions—moving home plate 20 feet closer to the distant outfield wall—he blasted 30 home runs in 1938. That total shattered Harry Heilmann's previous club record of 19 and ranked second in the NL to Mel Ott's 36.

With his bushy eyebrows and piercing glare, Goodman presented a fierce mien, more in keeping with an anarchist or bank robber than a ballplayer, which partly explains his being saddled with the moniker "Ival the Terrible." Fearless at the plate, he led the NL three times in being hit by pitched balls. A man of few words, Goodman was also inclined to settle disputes with fists, not talk. The deciding tally in the Yankees' 2–1 opening game win in the 1939 World Series was set up in the bottom of the ninth when Charlie Keller hit a long drive into right center between Harry Craft and Goodman. Ival lunged for the ball but couldn't corral it, and Keller wound up on third with a triple. One batter later, Keller trotted home on a single by Bill Dickey. Losing pitcher Paul Derringer screamed at Goodman in the distraught Reds' clubhouse for not making the catch. Goodman's response: a solid punch to Derringer's jaw.

The Reds, of course, would have been nowhere without Goodman, who made the NL All-Star team in 1938 and '39 and received votes for the NL MVP Award both years. His .323 average in '39 was the highest of his career. Manager Bill McKechnie regarded Goodman as the team's best all-around hitter, evidenced by the Deacon's slotting "Goodie" in the batting order's third spot for all 11 Series games played by the Reds in '39 and '40. Ival batted .333 in the first Series against New York and .276 in the second against Detroit with 5 RBI. His hitting might have been more robust had he not injured his shoulder while diving for a ball during the 1939 All-Star Game. His swing was never quite the same after that mishap.

Injuries continued to plague Goodman, and he finished up with two seasons as a Chicago Cub. He then managed in the minors, scouted for the Cubs, and sold chemicals for 25 years. He was elected to the Reds Hall of Fame in 1959, and a few months before his death in 1984 the baseball field at Carl Albert State College in Poteau, Oklahoma, was named in his honor.

YEAR	TM	G	AB	R	H	HR	RBI	SB	BB	SO	BA
1935–42	CIN (8 yrs)	965	3562	554	995	91	464	45	335	345	.279
1943–44	CHC (2 yrs)	142	366	55	109	4	61	4	47	35	.298
Total		1107	3928	609	1104	95	525	49	382	380	.281

Johnny Vander Meer

On the evening of June 15, 1938, a standing-room-only assemblage, including the recently retired Babe Ruth and Olympic hero Jesse Owens, jammed into Brooklyn's Ebbets Field for a game against Cincinnati. Other than a contingent of family and friends who came specifically to see the second-year Reds' pitcher from their town of Midland Park, New Jersey, the crowd was on hand for the ballpark's first night game ever. What the fans witnessed, in addition to the completely overshadowed inauguration of nocturnal baseball at Ebbets, was one of the most exciting and spectacular achievements in baseball history: the second of Johnny Vander Meer's consecutive no-hitters.

Four days earlier, the 24-year-old high-kicking left-hander had no-hit the Boston Bees 3–0 in an afternoon tilt at Crosley Field, but nobody on hand for Vandy's second masterpiece was expecting a repeat of the first game. After all, no major league pitcher had even tossed two no-hit games in the same season before, let alone back-to-back no-hitters.

Around the fifth inning when they realized what was happening, the rabidly parochial Dodgers' fans began rooting for Vander Meer, who didn't run into trouble until the ninth inning when, with one out, he walked the bases loaded. With every heart in the ballpark pounding with anxiety, Vandy calmed down after a few words from manager Bill McKecknie and finished the job, inducing Ernie Koy to ground out third to home for the second out and then coaxing Leo Durocher to loft a shallow fly ball that was easily caught by center fielder Harry Craft. Bedlam ensued at Ebbets, and "The Dutch Master," as Vander Meer was dubbed because his parents were immigrants from Holland, became an instant national celebrity.

As exciting as it was, the finish was symptomatic of Vander Meer's Achilles' heel: his inability to control his blazing fastball on a consistent basis.

Once the property of both teams he no-hit, Vander Meer toiled in the minors, at least partly, for seven seasons. His being named Minor League pitcher of the Year in 1936 for Durham and the strikeout record (295) he set there convinced the Reds he had superstar potential. In the spring of '38 the Reds hired Lefty Grove to help him with his control, and the tutoring seemed to pay off. Vandy went 15–10 on the season and seemed, after the double no-hit tour de force, poised to become a great pitcher; however, wildness and injuries hampered him the next two years and limited his contribution to the Reds' two pennant-winning campaigns to a combined eight wins (against 10 losses).

Speaking of John's frustrating and puzzling inconsistency, McKechnie said, "He was capable of periods of dazzling brilliance and then he would hit the other extreme and be absolutely ineffective." The "brilliant" Vandy struck out six batters in the 1943 All-Star Game in 2⅔ innings and recorded 30 shutouts among his 119 career wins, while the "ineffective" Vandy led the league in walks two times and totaled 1,132 free passes in 2,104 innings.

As the Reds' championship-quality squad slowly fell apart, Vander Meer put together the best run of his career (1941–43), winning 16, 18, and 15 games with ERAs of 2.82, 2.43, and 2.87, while leading the league in strikeouts each year. Vandy lost the next two years (1944–45) to WWII and had trouble regaining his form after the war. His final decent year came in 1948 when he went 17–14 with an ERA of 3.41. Upon retiring, he managed in the minors for 10 years before going into business in Tampa, Florida.

Career greatness eluded Johnny Vander Meer, but he gained immortality for a record that will never be broken. Lists of baseball's greatest moments never fail to include his double no-hit achievement.

YEAR	TM	W	L	ERA	GS	CG	SHO	IP	H	R	BB	SO
1937–49	CIN (11 yrs)	116	116	3.41	279	131	29	2028	1731	863	1072	1251
1950	CHC (1 yr)	3	4	3.79	6	0	0	73.2	60	46	59	41
1951	CLE (1 yr)	0	1	18.00	1	0	0	3	8	6	1	2
Total		119	121	3.44	286	131	29	2104.2	1799	915	1132	1294

Ewell Blackwell

He was six feet six and weighed maybe 190 pounds after a big meal. Red Smith said he looked like "a fly rod with ears." His windup, a whirling confusion of long arms and legs and big feet, was so deceptive that Braves' third baseman Bob Elliott said "it was like trying to hit an octopus." The blazing, sinking, side-armed fastball he threw from what seemed like the third base dugout terrified right-handed batters and earned him the sobriquet "The Whip." And for one season he was the most spectacular pitcher the Reds ever had.

As a 19-year-old pitching semipro ball in Downey, California, Ewell Blackwell attracted the attention of several big-league teams in 1942. The Reds were able to sign him because they were the only team willing to try him out in spring training. The Reds took Blackwell north and even let him pitch a few innings before farming him out to Syracuse in the top-flight International League. The kid was already so intimidating that teammates refused to take batting practice against him. He won 15 games for the Chiefs while posting an ERA of 2.02 and then pitched 30 shutout innings in the IL playoffs. He spent the next three years in Europe, serving with Patton's Third Army and winning two battle stars. He also pitched for the 71st Division, leading them to the Third Army Championship.

Blackwell's rookie record (9–13) with the Reds in 1946 was deceptive, considering that his five shutouts led the NL while his 2.46 ERA was fourth best. After a 2–2 start the next year, he turned into a monster on the mound. Blackwell reeled off a National League record (for right-handers) 16 straight wins, all complete games; went 22–8 on the year; and led the league in strikeouts with 193. Amazingly, in the middle of this streak he almost duplicated Johnny Vander Meer's famous accomplish-

ment. After no-hitting the Boston Braves on June 18, he no-hit the Brooklyn Dodgers for 8⅓ innings before Eddie Stanky lined a single through the box. "Blackie" finished the game with a two-hit shutout. In addition to these two gems, the streak included four three-hitters.

Alas, although Blackwell pitched in six straight All-Star Games (1946–51), running up a streak of 11 scoreless innings, injuries and health problems prevented him from maintaining such brilliance. A sore shoulder hampered him in 1948, while an operation to remove one of his kidneys before the season led to a mediocre record in '49. Ewell bounced back to notch 17 wins in 1950, and he flashed his former dominance with a two-hitter and a pair of one-hitters; but an emergency appendectomy set him back again toward the end of the season. A 16-win campaign in 1951 was his final big season.

Blackwell lost 12 of 15 decisions in 1952 for the Reds, who traded him on August 28 to the New York Yankees for four players. He pitched in only five games for New York but started the fifth game of the '52 World Series, going five innings and getting a no decision. After appearing in eight games for the Yankees in 1953 and two games for Kansas City in 1955, he retired from the game with a record of 82–78. He subsequently worked for large distilleries in Tampa and Columbia, South Carolina, and as a security guard. While Blackwell's career won-lost record is not exceptional, he made a deep and lasting impression on those who saw him pitch at his best. A panel of expert newspapermen picked him as the pitcher they'd want for the "ball game of their lives," and Waite Hoyt said, "There was a time when Blackie was as close to unbeatable as a pitcher can get."

YEAR	TM	W	L	ERA	GS	CG	SHO	IP	H	R	BB	SO
1942–52	CIN (8 yrs)	79	77	3.32	163	69	15	1281.1	1118	547	532	819
1952–53	NYY (2 yrs)	3	0	2.27	6	0	0	35.2	29	12	25	18
1955	KCA (1 yr)	0	1	6.75	0	0	0	4	3	3	5	2
Total		82	78	3.30	169	69	15	1321	1150	562	562	839

Joe Nuxhall

He began as the answer to a famous baseball trivia question and ended as a beloved civic icon. But long before he became the perpetual, soothing radio voice of summer for countless Reds' fans across the Midwest, he established himself in the major leagues as a tough competitor and one of the biggest winners in team history. Now he epitomizes the term Cincinnati Reds legend.

Joe Nuxhall started building his legend early as a local all-around sports star in Hamilton, Ohio, the sports-factory, Reds-crazy burg just outside of Cincinnati. Desperate for pitching during the roster-depleting days of WWII, the Reds wanted to sign Joe's dad as a pitcher, but Orville Nuxhall thought he needed to keep the job he had to take care of his growing family. The Reds instead signed the eldest Nuxhall son, who'd just finished ninth grade, placed him on the big league club, and shocked everyone, including Joe, by inserting him into a game in June 1944 as a reliever. Nuxhall lasted two-thirds of an inning against the Cardinals before his wildness compelled the Reds to relieve him. As brief as the 15-year-old's debut was, it showed two things: the kid had composure and he had a major league arm.

The Reds sent Nuxhall for seasoning to Birmingham, Alabama, beginning a six-year minor league odyssey that saw him also pitch in Syracuse, New York; Lima, Ohio; Muncie, Indiana; Columbia, South Carolina; Charleston, West Virginia; and Tulsa, Oklahoma. It took Nuxhall that long to get a grip on the two problems that held him back: his wildness and his volatile temper. He made the Reds out of spring training in 1952 as the last man working out of the bullpen. A three-inning scoreless stint in Brooklyn in late May finally solidified his spot on the team. A 1–4 record for the year was cushioned by his 3.22 ERA and his greatly improved control (49 walks in 92⅓ IP).

Nuxhall became a starter the next year and went 21–16 combined in 1953–54. When an overflow crowd showed up to celebrate a night for "Hamilton Joe," the Reds realized how popular Nuxhall was. He became the staff ace in '55, winning 17 games (third best in the NL) and leading the league in shutouts. He also made the All-Star team and was unscored on in 3⅓ innings.

After making the All-Star team again in '56, Nuxy became a .500 pitcher (31–30) through 1959. Booed unmercifully, he staggered to a 1–8 record in 1960 and was traded for his own good to Kansas City after the season. He returned to Cincinnati in early '62 and posted his best overall campaign in 1963, going 15–8 with 169 strikeouts and an ERA of 2.61. He capped his career with an 11–4 mark in 1965 and finished 135–117 lifetime, all but five of the wins coming as a Red. He retired with the third most strikeouts (1,289) in team history.

Nuxhall went into the Reds' radio booth in 1967. He teamed up with Marty Brennaman in 1974, and for the next 30 years the pair, who became best friends, treated Reds' fans to broadcasts as entertaining as the action on the field: Joe's enthusiastic home-team boosterism serving as the perfect complement to Marty's glib, candid professionalism. As the years passed and players came and went, Nuxhall became the face of the franchise. Involving himself in numerous charities, he inspired thousands of others to follow his example. A member of the Reds Hall of Fame since 1968, he lived to see his statue erected outside Great American Ball Park, which bears the key part of his radio sign-off in neon lights: "This is the old lefthander *rounding third and heading for home.*"

YEAR	TM	W	L	ERA	GS	CG	SHO	IP	H	R	BB	SO
1944 1952–60 1962–66	CIN (15 yrs)	130	109	3.80	274	82	20	2169.1	2168	1006	706	1289
1961	KCA (1 yr)	5	8	5.34	13	1	0	128	135	81	65	81
1962	LAA (1 yr)	0	0	10.13	0	0	0	5.1	7	6	5	2
Total		135	117	3.90	287	83	20	2302.2	2310	1093	776	1372

Ted Kluszewski

New York Giants' manager Leo Durocher once referred to Gil Hodges as the strongest player in baseball, causing a reporter to ask about Cincinnati's first baseman. "Kluszewski?" exclaimed Durocher, "I'm talking about *human beings!*"

Hodges *was* a he-man, but there was no player in baseball in the 1950s more powerful than Theodore Bernard Kluszewski, a Hercules in flannel whose muscles, it was said, had muscles of their own. Klu's bulging biceps and massive chest endowed him with the physique of a superhero, and he exuded the dignified swagger of John Wayne (a movie star Kluszewski admired) playing a tough hombre. Klu's big arms even brought about a uniform innovation. When nobody did anything about his complaints that the sleeves of his jersey were restricting his swing, Klu cut the sleeves off himself, thus freeing his movements and inventing a jersey style the Reds later adopted for the entire team.

Kluszewski was also a dangerous hitter, literally. He once shot back toward the mound a line drive so fierce it struck Phillies' pitcher Bubba Church in the face, opening a horrendous cut on Church's cheek and dislodging his eyeball. Fortunately, while Klu was physically intimidating, he was a gentle, humble, friendly man.

Big Klu could have played professional football, as he had been an All-American end as a sophomore for the Big Ten Champion Indiana University. Bloomington, in fact, is where the Reds discovered him when they trained there during WWII. As a reward for helping prepare the practice diamond, Klu was allowed to take batting practice in front of the major leaguers. Mouths dropped open when his blasts soared far beyond any distance reached by Reds' players.

With the Reds, the left-handed Kluszewski became one of the most feared sluggers in the National League. Over a four-year period (1953–56) he averaged 43 home runs and 116 RBI. His biggest year came in 1954 when he set team records for home runs (49), RBI (141), and slugging percentage (.642), while batting .326 to finish second in the MVP voting behind Willie Mays. At the time, only six other players had homered 50 or more times in one season, and some observers think that Klu's failure to join the 50-HR club cost him the recognition he deserved.

On the other hand, Kluszewski could do more than just hit the long ball. The batting champion of two different minor leagues, he batted over .300 seven times for Cincinnati and was harder to strike out than most pesky leadoff hitters. In 1954 when he hit 49 homers, he struck out only 35 times. He clouted 47 taters the next year and whiffed 40 times. In his 15-year major league career, he hit 279 home runs and struck out 365 times, giving him the third lowest strikeout/home run ratio of all time (minimum 200 career HRs) behind Joe DiMaggio and Yogi Berra. While he didn't have the greatest range, Klu was an expert at digging out low throws, and he led NL first basemen in fielding percentage five years in a row. He batted .500 (7–14) in four All-Star Game appearances.

Klu's chronic back injury prompted the Reds to trade him to Pittsburgh after the '57 season, precipitating the final stage of his career. His last hurrah came in the 1959 World Series with the Chicago White Sox, for whom he batted .391 with 10 RBI and three home runs.

Kluszewski later maintained his status as a Cincinnati baseball icon by serving as the Reds' batting coach for years. He was as beloved by his pupils as he had been by his teammates. Today his statue outside Great American Ball Park is a magnet for moms and dads with cameras.

YEAR	TM	G	AB	R	H	HR	RBI	SB	BB	SO	BA
1947–57	CIN (11 yrs)	1339	4961	745	1499	251	886	20	406	292	.302
1958–59	PIT (2 yrs)	160	423	40	120	6	54	0	31	30	.284
1959–60	CHW (2 yrs)	112	282	31	83	7	49	0	31	20	.294
1961	LAA (1 yr)	107	263	32	64	15	39	0	24	23	.243
Total		1718	5929	848	1766	279	1028	20	492	365	.298

1951–1975

Wally Post

He was shy and unassuming. Just an "easy-going, regular guy," according to his best friend, Joe Nuxhall. But he was also "bull strong" and could hit a baseball a country mile. He became a key member of the "Western Avenue Bombers" who knocked down the walls of Crosley Field in the summer of 1956, and Reds' fans loved him.

The Reds signed Walter Charles Post, a hotshot pitcher, out of St. Henry, Ohio, near the Indiana border. Right after graduating from high school in 1946, "Wally" made his professional debut at age 16 with Middletown (OH) of the Class D Ohio State League. The next year in the same league, Post went 17–7 for Muncie, Indiana. Teammate Nuxhall was certain that Post would beat him to the big leagues as a pitcher, but because of Post's .338 batting average the Reds began re-assessing Wally's future. Post made the switch to the outfield in 1949 with Charleston, West Virginia, of the Central League.

After several late-season cups of coffee, Post proved he was ready for The Show by slugging 33 HRs with 120 RBI for Indianapolis in 1953. As a rookie right fielder with Cincinnati, Post appeared in 130 games, batting .255 with 18 HRs and 83 RBI. Wally laughed at the sophomore jinx in 1955, as he turned in what would be the best season of his career: a .309 average in 154 games with 40 long balls, 116 runs, and 109 RBI. Post's 40 HRs combined with Ted Kluszewski's 47 established the Reds' best two-man total ever.

In 1956 the name Wally Post became as familiar in American households as the well-known breakfast cereal. Wally's batting average dipped to .249, but he hit 36 more homers—including four in a doubleheader on April 29—and home runs were the story in Rhineland

that summer. Lead by Frank Robinson (38), Post, and Kluszewski (35), the Reds pounded 221 balls over the fences to tie the major league record. After years of mediocrity, the Reds were in a pennant race, the team drew over a million fans for the first time, and the national spotlight was suddenly shining on the Cincinnati Redlegs.

In June, Post appeared with seven teammates on the television program *What's My Line?* (and stumped the panel of Bennett Cerf, Arlene Francis, and Dorothy Kilgallen, by the way) while a few weeks later Post found himself, along with Kluszewski and Gus Bell, on the cover of the July 16 issue of *Sports Illustrated*.

Post hit 20 or more home runs in a season three more times and finished with 210 homers, 171 of them as a Red. Those totals are not impressive today, but many of Post's home runs were. No other Red has hit as many tape-measure jobs as Post.

In 1961 he crushed the hardest-hit ball in franchise history. The missile, which crashed into the scoreboard clock at old Busch Stadium in St. Louis, would have traveled 569 feet had its flight not been interrupted, according to Reds' pitcher Jay Hook, who earned a degree in engineering from Northwestern. Because of his long home runs, Post also became famous for his wardrobe, compliments of Siebler Tailors. Wally hit the haberdashery's "Hit Sign, Win Suit" target atop the laundry beyond the left field wall at Crosley Field a record 11 times in 12 seasons.

The Reds traded Post to Philadelphia after the 1957 season but got him back in time for the 1961 pennant run. He contributed 20 HRs and 57 RBI to the cause and then hit .333 with a home run in the Series against the Yankees. Post died of cancer in 1982 at the age of 52.

YEAR	TM	G	AB	R	H	HR	RBI	SB	BB	SO	BA
1949, 1951–57 1960–63	CIN (12 yrs)	902	3021	463	805	172	525	19	249	593	.266
1958–60	PHP (3 yrs)	276	931	124	250	36	168	0	77	199	.269
1963	MIN (1 yr)	21	47	6	9	2	6	0	2	17	.191
1964	CLE (1 yr)	5	8	1	0	0	0	0	3	4	.000
Total		1204	4007	594	1064	210	699	19	331	813	.266

Gus Bell

Branch Rickey, the visionary who engineered Jackie Robinson's integration of the major leagues, had a reputation as the shrewdest man in baseball. Nobody ever outwitted him in a trade, except the time the Reds got Rickey, general manager of the Pirates, to part with a cocky young outfielder named David Russell Bell. Years later, after Bell had become a four-time NL All-Star for Cincinnati, the Mahatma admitted that "it was the worst trade I ever made."

A high school catcher in Louisville, Kentucky, Bell was nicknamed "Gus" after New York Giants' backstop Gus Mancuso. Bell was signed by the Pittsburgh Pirates, who made him a center fielder because he had all five tools. He shot through the minor leagues and got the call to the Steel City in May 1950 after hitting .400 the first six weeks of the season in Indianapolis. Gus hit .282 in 111 games for the Bucs that rookie season.

He had a solid year in '51 (.278/16/89) while leading the league in triples, but then he landed in Rickey's doghouse for demanding a raise and ignoring the old man's prohibition against traveling with family to spring training games. Bell's off year in 1952 (.250) made it easier for Rickey to unload him to the Reds that winter.

With the Reds, Bell immediately blossomed into one of the best players in the league. Crediting unpopular Cincinnati manager Rogers Hornsby with improving his approach at the plate by teaching him to hit up the middle, Gus hit .300 with 105 RBI and a career-high 30 HRs. Bell batted over .290 for five of the next six seasons and knocked in more than 100 runs three more times with a high of 115 in 1959. He also set a Reds' record for most putouts by a center fielder (447), led NL center fielders in

fielding percentage twice, and set a major-league record for consecutive errorless games with 200. Such reliability prompted Reds' manager Birdie Tebbets to say, "He's so remarkably steady, he sometimes goes unnoticed."

Despite his consistency, Bell was also at times a one-man wrecking crew. He is one of only three Reds' players to hit three HRs in a game twice, and on three other occasions he racked up eight RBI in a single day (twice in doubleheaders and once in a single game).

In 1957 Reds' fans got a little carried away in the famous "stuffing of the ballot box" incident which initially resulted in Redlegs winning the vote for seven of the eight positions in the starting lineup of the National League All-Star team. Commissioner Ford Frick stepped in and replaced Wally Post and Bell with Willie Mays and Hank Aaron, but NL manager Walter Alston put Gus back on the team as a reserve. Bell justified Alston's faith in him by hitting a two-run pinch-hit double in the game.

With the arrival of Vada Pinson and then Gordy Coleman, Bell was shifted first to right field and later into a platoon situation. During the scintillating 1961 season he appeared in 103 games and batted only three times during the World Series against New York. After the Series he went to the fledgling New York Mets in the expansion draft and had the distinction of getting the first hit, a single, in team history. He entered the Reds Hall of Fame in 1964, having posted a .288 career average as a Red with 1,343 hits, 160 HRs, and 711 RBI.

Bell's son, Buddy, who enjoyed a fine career as a third baseman, played for the Reds; and when his son, David, also donned a Reds' uniform, the Bells became the only three-generation family to play for one team.

YEAR	TM	G	AB	R	H	HR	RBI	SB	BB	SO	BA
1950–52	PIT (3 yrs)	391	1490	195	403	40	201	6	106	159	.270
1953–61	CIN (9 yrs)	1235	4667	634	1343	160	711	24	342	452	.288
1962	NYM (1 yr)	30	101	8	15	1	6	0	10	7	.149
1962–64	MIL (3 yrs)	85	220	28	62	5	24	0	12	18	.318
Total		1741	6478	865	1823	206	942	30	470	636	.281

Frank Robinson

On December 9, 1965, the Reds made the worst miscalculation since Custer started that ill-advised brawl at Little Bighorn: trading one of the greatest sluggers in baseball history in the prime of his career to the Baltimore Orioles for three journeyman players. General manager Bill Dewitt justified the trade of outfielder Frank Robinson by describing him as an "old thirty." Robby destroyed that characterization by having the best year of his life in 1966, copping the American League Triple Crown (.316/49/122) and MVP Award, leading the Orioles to the World Championship, and leaving Reds' fans to forever wonder how many more pennants Cincinnati may have won had Robinson amassed all of his 586 HRs and 1,812 RBI in the city where he started his career.

The Reds had no trouble recognizing Robinson's talent in the beginning, scouting him as a 14-year-old in Oakland, California. After his 1953 graduation from McClymonds High School, where he played basketball with Bill Russell, Robinson bounded through the Reds' minor-league system and became an immediate big-league star, winning the 1956 NL Rookie of the Year Award for blasting a record-tying 38 HRs.

Except for 1963 when he was hampered more than usual by injuries, Robinson never had a bad year for the Reds. Over his 10-year career in Cincinnati, Robinson batted .303, averaged 33 HRs, and racked up 100+ runs and 90+ RBI six times each. He led the NL in slugging percentage three years in a row (1960–62), won the NL MVP Award in 1961, left town as the all-time Reds' (324) and Crosley Field (176) home run leader, and was named to the NL All-Star team six times (he made the AL All-Star team six times as well).

As impressive as his stats were, Robinson was even more respected (by most people) for the fierce way he played the game. Infielders feared his aggressive sliding; he led the Reds into several major brawls; and at bat he crowded the plate fearlessly, his head and upper body hanging over the dish in what Earl Weaver described as his "death-defying stance." Robinson was brushed back constantly and hit by pitches often, but such tactics only served to intensify his determination to succeed and defeat the opponent.

Robinson was an introvert and a loner—at least until Vada Pinson joined the Reds and became his roommate—and a bit misunderstood at times. As the Reds' first black star, he was a direct beneficiary of Jackie Robinson's trailblazing, as well as a magnet for lingering racism. The turning point in his life and career came in 1960 when he was arrested for brandishing a handgun during an ugly confrontation in a Cincinnati hamburger joint. Realizing that he needed to be a better role model for the thousands of kids who idolized him, Robinson apologized for the incident and vowed to grow up and rededicate himself to being the best player he could be. His MVP performance that summer led the Reds to their first pennant in two decades.

The Orioles went to four World Series during Robinson's six years in Baltimore, and in 1972 after they had traded him to the Dodgers, they retired his number—26 years before the Reds did the same thing.

Robinson padded his Hall of Fame stats by playing one season for the Dodgers and two for the Angels and then became a trailblazer himself by signing on as the player-manager of the Cleveland Indians. His first-inning home run on April 8, 1975, helped make his debut a winning one. He later also managed the Giants, Orioles, and Expos and worked in several different high-level front-office capacities for major-league baseball.

YEAR	TM	G	AB	R	H	HR	RBI	SB	BB	SO	BA
1956–65	CIN (10 yrs)	1502	5527	1043	1673	324	1009	161	698	789	.303
1966–71	BAL (6 yrs)	827	2941	555	882	179	545	35	460	452	.300
1972	LAD (1 yr)	103	342	41	86	19	59	2	55	76	.251
1973–74	CAL (2 yrs)	276	961	160	249	50	160	6	157	178	.259
1974–76	CLE (3 yrs)	100	235	30	53	14	39	0	50	37	.226
Total		2808	10006	1829	2943	586	1812	204	1420	1532	.294

Vada Pinson

Being forecast as the "next Mickey Mantle" is a heavy burden to lay on any young baseball hopeful, and the label often pressures the bearer into failure, at least temporarily. Because he appeared to exhibit the Mick's rare combination of power and speed, center fielder Vada Pinson is one Cincinnati Reds legend who got stuck with the troublesome appellation. Fortunately, he not only survived it but carved out for himself a glittering career as one of the best players of his generation.

Coming out of the same Oakland, California, high school that produced Bill Russell, Frank Robinson, and Curt Flood, Vada Edward Pinson was probably used to heightened expectations from the beginning. He certainly wasted little time in living up to them, forcing himself into the Reds' 1958 Opening Day lineup after only one season in the minors at Class C Visalia, California. Hitting a grand slam in his second major-league game caused him to start overswinging and soon led to his demotion to Seattle of the Pacific Coast League for the rest of the season. Back for good the next year, the left-handed hitting and throwing Pinson played in every game on the Reds' schedule and turned in a performance that would have won him the NL Rookie of the Year Award had he not been ineligible because he'd accumulated a couple of ABs too many the year before. Vada batted .316 with 20 HRs, 84 RBI, and 21 stolen bases, while leading the league in at bats (648), runs (131), doubles (47), and OF putouts (423). He also became only the fourth player in history to collect more than 200 hits in his first full season.

Pinson never demonstrated the long-distance power of Mantle, but he did have all five tools at his disposal, especially speed to burn, which made him a danger-ous hitter, bunter, and base runner, capable of exerting constant pressure on the defense. An outstanding fielder who made numerous circus catches, he won the Gold Glove in 1961 and led the league in putouts two more times. Nothing proved his all-around ability more than the totals he averaged for the first five years of his career: 197 hits, a .310 average, 108 runs, 37 doubles, 20 HRs, 88 RBI, and 26 stolen bases. He led the NL in doubles in 1960 (37), and in triples and hits twice. He batted over .300 three more times, with a high of .343 in 1961 that placed him second, behind batting champion Roberto Clemente, and in 1965 he enjoyed separate hitting streaks of 27 and 23 games.

Pinson was roommates and best friends with Frank Robinson, and until Robinson was traded to Baltimore they combined for as formidable a one-two punch as any in the NL. Robinson did hit the long ball, and it was he, in fact, who overshadowed Pinson. Even after Robinson's departure, Pinson did not become the biggest star on the team because a brash young second baseman named Pete Rose came along to soak up most of the attention. Not that the quiet, gentlemanly Pinson cared. He simply showed up each day ready to do his best. Pinson played 154 games or more for the Reds for nine straight years and put together one streak of 508 consecutive games.

A chronic hamstring pull finally caught up with Pinson in 1968, and the Reds dealt him to St. Louis where he played one year, before finishing his career in the American League with three different teams. The proud owner of 2,757 hits, 256 HRs, and 305 stolen bases, he coached in the majors for 16 years and died of a stroke in 1995 at age 57 in his hometown of Oakland.

YEAR	TM	G	AB	R	H	HR	RBI	SB	BB	SO	BA
1958–68	CIN (11 yrs)	1565	6335	978	1881	186	814	221	409	831	.297
1969	STL (1 yr)	132	495	58	126	10	70	4	35	63	.255
1970–71	CLE (2 yrs)	294	1140	134	313	35	117	32	49	127	.275
1972–73	CAL (2 yrs)	260	950	112	254	15	106	22	50	109	.267
1974–75	KCR (2 yrs)	218	725	84	183	10	63	26	31	66	.252
Total		2469	9645	1366	2757	256	1170	305	574	1196	.286

Jim Maloney

The fastest pitcher in Cincinnati Reds' history didn't even pitch on his high school team. When he started in pro ball in 1959, he was so raw the rubes of the Class B Three-I League beat him like a drum. Yet a few years later he'd become a strikeout dynamo, a threat to toss a no-hitter for the Reds every time out, and only injuries prevented him from taking his place among the immortals in Cooperstown.

Like two other great Reds' pitchers (Ewell Blackwell and Tom Seaver), Jim Maloney was born in Fresno, California, where he played shortstop on the local high school nine because Dick Ellsworth, who later pitched for the Chicago Cubs, was the squad's mound ace. Reds' scout Bobby Mattick convinced Maloney to switch to pitching and signed him for a bonus of $100,000, a huge sum of money in 1959.

Johnny Vander Meer (in Topeka) and Jim Turner (in San Diego) taught Maloney how to pitch, and the fireballing right-hander made his Reds' debut after only a season and a half in the minors. Wildness limited Maloney to 15 wins combined in 1961 and '62, but the following year he burst into stardom, going 23–7 with an ERA of 2.77 and 265 strikeouts. He won in double figures for the next six seasons, with a high of 20 in 1965, and he led the Reds in ERA three times and strikeouts five times.

Maloney's blazing fastball (clocked at 99.5 mph in 1965), combined with his wildness, struck fear into the hearts of batters. When he was able to get his curveball over the plate, he was unhittable. He did, in fact, throw three no-hitters, although baseball today does not recognize his 10 innings of no-hit ball against the Mets on June 14, 1965, because he lost the no-hitter and the game in the 11th inning on a home run by Johnny Lewis. Two

months after the Mets' game, Maloney repeated his magic against the Cubs at Wrigley Field, again having to no-hit the opposition for 10 innings to get the 1–0 win. The Reds did seem to have trouble scoring runs for Maloney, and after his gem against the Cubs, sportswriter Jim Murray joked about his hard luck, saying the Maloney family coat of arms should be "a field of black cats rampant on a shield of snake-eyed dice." Maloney's third no-hitter was a bit easier, as the Reds beat Houston at Crosley in a 10–0 laugher on April 30, 1969.

Maloney's dominance was further evident in his high-strikeout games. He tied the team record for Ks in one game on May 21, 1963, when he whiffed 16 Braves, eight of them in a row, and in the 10-inning no-hitter against the Mets he struck out 18. In addition to the no-hitters, Maloney chalked up five one-hitters, 10 two-hitters, and 30 shutouts. Maloney was also a good hitter, evidenced by a .379 average in 1961, 13 RBI in 73 at bats in 1964, and seven career home runs.

Unfortunately, Maloney's power pitching led to his downfall, as it put tremendous stress on his body and tore, rather than stretched, the muscles in his arm. Typically high-pitch counts, numerous walks, and nagging injuries and sore arms were also detrimental to his longevity. The fatal blow was a torn Achilles tendon that cost Maloney the 1970 season, prompting his trade to the Angels after the season, and essentially ended his career.

Maloney later overcame his own problems with the bottle to work as the director of an alcohol/drug abuse center in Fresno, and today he is remembered fondly as the Reds' all-time strikeout leader with 1,592 and as a most worthy member of the team's Hall of Fame.

YEAR	TM	W	L	ERA	GS	CG	SHO	IP	H	R	BB	SO
1960–70	CIN (11 yrs)	134	81	3.16	258	74	30	1818.2	1483	711	786	1592
1971	CAL (1 yr)	0	3	5.04	4	0	0	30.1	35	18	24	13
Total		134	84	3.19	262	74	30	1849	1518	729	810	1605

Pete Rose

When Whitey Ford and Mickey Mantle watched an unknown Reds' rookie in a meaningless spring-training game race to first base after a walk, as if he were running through fire in a gasoline suit, they thought they were seeing an act and asked sarcastically, "Who's that guy, 'Charlie Hustle'?"

The player was Peter Edward Rose. Hometown: Cincinnati, Ohio. And his all-out/all-the-time approach wasn't a fraud then, any more than it was later when he ran over American League catcher Ray Fosse to score the winning run in the 1970 All-Star Game or when, taking an extra base on an outfielder's bobble, he flew headfirst into third base to a thundering ovation during his first game in a Reds' uniform as player-manager after his exile to Philadelphia and Montreal.

A scrawny river rat signed by the Reds as a favor to a relative connected to the team, Rose filled out nicely after high school and hustled and hit his way quickly through the Reds' farm system. To the chagrin of veteran players, manager Fred Hutchinson, who admired Rose's aggressiveness, burning desire, and unerring baseball instincts, gave the raw kid the Reds' second base job in 1963. Rose grabbed the opportunity with both hands and never looked back. He won the NL Rookie of the Year Award, cracking the first 170 of his eventual total of 4,256 hits, the all-time major-league record.

How did the switch-hitting Rose become the "Hit King"? By playing every day (he ranks first in games played), by never giving up an at bat, and by constantly stoking a desire to squeeze the benefit out of every ounce of his ability.

In 1965 Rose hit .312 and led the league in hits with 209. He would bat over .300 14 more times and accumulate 200 or more hits in a season nine more times. He won batting titles in 1968, '69, and '73 and the NL MVP Award in 1973. His 44-game hitting streak in 1978 thrilled the nation and set the record for the National League.

Rose was integral to the success of the Big Red Machine, and he put the team first by playing defensively and playing well, wherever the team needed him. His unselfish move from left field to third base in order for the Reds to get George Foster's bat into the lineup was the piece that completed the Reds' World Championships puzzle of 1975–76. After signing as a free agent with Philadelphia, Rose played first base the rest of his career. That switch resulted in his starting NL All-Star Games at five different positions (2B, RF, LF, 3B, 1B), an unmatched record of versatility. He played in 16 All-Star Games total and was also the only player in history to play more than 500 games at four different positions.

Rose set far too many records to mention over his 24-year career (itself a NL record); however, as records-conscious as he was, Rose did not play for personal statistics. He played to win and frequently reminds fans that he holds the major-league record for having played in the most winning games (1,972). His desire to win was contagious too. Phillies' players have always credited him with teaching their formerly underachieving squads how to win, and players on the Reds' 1990 World Championship team have acknowledged that Rose, in the previous four years as their manager, laid the foundation for their ultimate success.

Rose made a terrible mistake by betting on baseball, and his punishment continues to be his ineligibility for Cooperstown. But no one doubts that his incomparable record on the diamond makes him a de facto Hall of Famer of the first rank.

YEAR	TM	G	AB	R	H	HR	RBI	SB	BB	SO	BA
1963–78 1984–86	CIN (19 yrs)	2722	10934	1741	3358	152	1036	146	1210	972	.307
1979–83	PHP (5 yrs)	745	2841	390	826	8	255	51	325	151	.291
1984	MON (1 yr)	95	278	34	72	0	23	1	31	20	.259
Total		3562	14053	2165	4256	160	1314	198	1566	1143	.303

Tony Perez

Reds' manager Dave Bristol said about him, "If the game goes on long enough, Tony Perez will find a way to win it." Catfish Hunter found out the truth of that statement the hard way when Perez, in his first of seven All-Star Game appearances, hit a 15th-inning home run off him to win the 1967 Summer Classic for the National League. Perez also tutored Bill Lee in a crucial situation, clubbing a key two-run, sixth-inning home run off him to get the Reds back into Game 7 of the '75 World Series.

Born May 14, 1942, in Ciego de Avila, Cuba, Atanasio Perez Rigal was a clutch hitter and RBI machine, whose ill-advised trade to Montreal after the 1976 season has come to symbolize the dismantling of the Big Red Machine.

The Reds signed the 17-year-old Perez off a Cuban sugar factory team in 1960 for a $2.50 visa and a plane ticket to Miami. He started his pro career in Geneva, New York, of the New York–Penn League where he made a lifelong friend in teammate Pete Rose. While overcoming difficulties with the culture and the language, the unflappable Perez moved steadily up the ladder until he earned a promotion to the Reds in 1964, the same year he was named MVP of the Pacific Coast League. He platooned at first base for a couple of years before the Reds converted him into the regular third baseman in 1967.

In 1970 Perez had his best overall year (.317/40/129), finishing third in the NL MVP voting, and in 1972 he became the Reds' regular first baseman. "Doggie," as Tony's teammates affectionately called him, drove in more than 100 runs for the Reds six times, and in a 10-year stretch (1967–1976) he never knocked in fewer than 90 Reds' base runners a year. Such a record of consistent production should have made a trade of the extremely popular Perez unthinkable, but it didn't.

The Reds were willing to part with Perez because they believed that the younger Dan Driessen would be an adequate replacement, and he may have been; however, they underestimated Perez's importance to the team's chemistry and to its psyche. Tony was a master needler, whose wit and sharp tongue kept the egos of other star players in check, and after his departure the Big Red Machine clubhouse was never the same again.

Perez had some good seasons for the Expos and the Red Sox, and he played a backup role on the Phillies' World Championship team of 1983 before he returned to Cincinnati for three final years as a part-time player. In 1984 he became the oldest player (42) to hit a walk-off pinch-hit homer, and the next year he became the oldest player to hit a grand slam. He retired with the second-most RBI (1,192) in Reds' history and the third-most home runs (287), and he remains ranked in the Reds' Top 5 in five other traditional batting categories. His 379 career home runs tied him at the time for the most by a Latin American player.

Hired to manage the Reds in 1993, Perez was abruptly fired after 44 games. He later managed the Florida Marlins briefly and still serves that team in a front-office capacity. For a while the sportswriters seemed to lack appreciation for Perez too, but the increasingly miffed "Big Dog" finally gained election to the Hall of Fame in his ninth year on the ballot. In his joyous, gracious speech, he said he carried the flags of three countries (America, Puerto Rico, and Cuba) in his heart but especially loved the city of Cincinnati, where the fans had never booed him. In other words, Reds' fans had never underestimated or failed to appreciate him.

YEAR	TM	G	AB	R	H	HR	RBI	SB	BB	SO	BA
1964–76 1984–86	CIN (16 yrs)	1948	6846	936	1934	287	1192	39	671	1306	.283
1977–79	MON (3 yrs)	434	1592	192	448	46	242	8	139	297	.281
1980–82	BOS (3 yrs)	304	1087	126	289	40	175	1	87	207	.266
1983	PHP (1 yr)	91	253	18	61	6	43	1	28	57	.241
Total		2777	9778	1272	2732	379	1652	49	925	1867	.279

Johnny Bench

The luckiest day in Cincinnati Reds' history came in June 1965 when a high school catcher out of Binger, Oklahoma, whom the Reds' brass liked, was still on the draft board when the team's second-round pick came around. That's because the kid named Johnny Lee Bench would go on to surpass everyone's expectations except his own. And when his 17-year career, all of it spent with the Reds, was over, he was accorded the rare honor of being regarded as having been the best in history to play his position.

If ever a player was born to be a major leaguer, it was Johnny Bench. His father groomed him from childhood to believe he had a special baseball destiny, and Bench was so sold on the idea he practiced his penmanship as a Little Leaguer in order that his future autographs would be legible.

Ted Bench believed that playing catcher was the quickest way to the big leagues, and in his son's case he was certainly correct. The big-boned huge-handed Bench made his debut with the Reds in 1967 at the end of this third pro season, and the next year he won the National League Rookie of the Year Award. Veterans were amazed at how talented, polished, and poised the young Bench was. In just his third season in the majors, Bench put on the most spectacular batting display ever seen by a catcher, averaging .293 with 45 HRs and a team-record 148 RBI. He won the 1972 NL MVP Award for his efforts, and two years later he won the award again for hitting .270 with 40 HRs and 125 RBI.

Amazingly, Bench was just as sensational behind the plate. An expert at every aspect of the catching position, he was especially adept at catching pop-ups, making sweep tags, and blocking the plate. He handled Reds' pitchers beautifully and completely shut down opposing teams' running games with the most powerful and accurate throwing arm a catcher had ever displayed.

Bench's development into one of baseball's biggest stars coincided with the rise of the Big Red Machine and gave Johnny numerous chances to shine in the spotlight. He homered in his first All-Star Game at bat in 1969, his leadoff ninth-inning game-tying home run (one of the most exciting HRs in team history) in the deciding game of the playoffs led the Reds to the 1972 pennant, and his performance in the 1976 World Series (.533 with two HRs), for which he was named MVP, almost single-handedly demolished the Yankees.

In 1977 Bench drove in more than 100 runs for the sixth and final time of his career, and he won his 10th consecutive and final Gold Glove Award for fielding excellence. After that his playing time and effectiveness began to decline as injuries and the demands of the position began to take their toll, and he played more and more games at first and third bases.

Nevertheless, the thrills kept coming. In 1979 with HR #314 Bench became the all-time HR King among catchers. When he hit #325 on August 22, he became the Reds' HR King. On May 29, 1980, Johnny hit three HRs in a game at San Diego, marking the third time in his career he'd cracked three long balls in one game. And in a fitting, emotionally charged conclusion for a player who'd been so clutch throughout his career, Bench hit his final home run at Riverfront Stadium on Johnny Bench Night when he made his official farewell to Reds' fans.

Bench set many records and has enjoyed far too many honors to enumerate. His legacy is that he changed the game and did it with class and integrity.

YEAR	TM	G	AB	R	H	HR	RBI	SB	BB	SO	BA
1967–83	CIN (17 yrs)	2158	7658	2048	1091	389	1376	68	891	1278	.267

Don Gullett

He sounded too good to be true: the kid from the little town in rural Greenup County, Kentucky, a place so small that nobody had ever heard of it; a natural three-sport star who'd scored 72 points in one football game and 47 points in one basketball game for Southshore McKell High School. Maybe the kid looked so good because the competition was weak. Reds' scout Cliff Alexander knew better after he'd watched the senior left-hander strike out 20 of 21 batters with nothing but a smoking fastball. "Better than Sandy Koufax at the same age," was the report Alexander turned in on Donald Edward Gullett.

The Reds made the Kentucky Kid their number one pick in the June 1969 amateur draft, and the very next year, after only 11 games in the minor leagues, Gullett was in Cincinnati, strutting out of the Reds' bullpen to throw what Willie Stargell later called "wall to wall heat." Gullett's five wins and a 2.43 ERA as a rookie plus two saves in the 1970 National League Championship Series made the Reds realize that they had discovered, in their own backyard no less, a young stud not only capable of joining the starting rotation but also of becoming the ace of the Cincinnati pitching staff—a worthy successor to Jim Maloney.

After pitching coach Larry Shepard helped him sharpen his curveball, Gullett became one of the NL's biggest winners the very next year. His 16–6 record led the league in winning percentage, and he would remain among the league leaders in that category on an almost yearly basis. He also became a favorite of manager Sparky Anderson, who started predicting that Gullett would wind up in the National Baseball Hall of Fame. Gullett won a career-high 18 games in 1973, and the following year, despite a back injury, he threw a career-high 243 innings while winning 17.

Don never did turn in a 20-win season, but he probably would have in 1975 and in 1976 had not a thumb injury in '75 and a pinched nerve in his neck and shoulder problems in '76 not limited him to 22 and 23 starts, respectively. Nevertheless, he went a combined 26–7 over the two years and won games in both the '75 and '76 World Series.

Gullett found contract negotiations to be unpleasant, and he'd always felt underpaid by the Reds. Consequently, he became one of the first players to hire an agent and to play out his option, which he did in 1976. A free agent at the end of the year, he signed a six-year deal with the New York Yankees worth $2 million, considered back then to be an outlandish salary for a baseball player.

The Reds were willing to let Gullett go because they disdained the free agent market and eschewed long-term contracts but also because they felt Gullett was damaged goods. They knew that Gullett's shoulder problems, due initially to his unnatural across-the-body throwing motion, had been exacerbated by an injury he suffered in February 1976 while competing in ABC's *The Superstars* competition in Hawaii.

Sure enough, while Gullett had one good year (14–4) for New York in 1977, the bad shoulder became an impassable roadblock on his road to Cooperstown. Dr. Frank Jobe operated on his torn rotator cuff the next year without success, so Gullett was forced to prematurely hang up his spikes. He retired at age 26 with a career ERA of 3.11 and a record of 109–50 for a winning percentage of .686, at the time the fourth-best percentage in baseball history. He later enjoyed a long stint (1993–2005) as the Reds' pitching coach and was inducted into the Reds Hall of Fame in 2002.

YEAR	TM	W	L	ERA	GS	CG	SHO	IP	H	R	BB	SO
1970–76	CIN (7 yrs)	91	44	3.03	156	35	13	1187	1022	442	412	777
1977–78	NYY (2 yrs)	18	6	3.59	30	9	1	203	183	86	89	144
Total		109	50	3.11	186	44	14	1390	1205	528	501	921

Joe Morgan

At five feet seven and 150 pounds, young Joe Morgan didn't look like a major-league ballplayer to the skeptics. Pitchers acted insulted whenever he took them deep, and Philadelphia manager Gene Mauch even referred to the rookie disgustedly as a "Little Leaguer" after Morgan had slapped a game-winning hit against the Phillies. Most people could not see that Morgan had the tools and the heart necessary to be the game's most dominant player, which is exactly what he became after the Houston Astros and the Reds completed the most important trade in Cincinnati history.

Born in Bonham, Texas, Morgan grew up in Oakland, California. He signed with the expansion Houston Colt 45s because their scout, unlike scouts with other teams, never mentioned any doubts about "Little Joe's" size. During brief trials in 1963 and '64, Morgan was encouraged by another diminutive second baseman, Nellie Fox, who was on the Houston roster partly in order to mentor Morgan. Morgan earned the regular second-base job in 1965 and in six full seasons with Houston hit .263 with an average of 10 HRs, 46 RBI, and 32 stolen bases. Not bad, but certainly not enough to make Reds' fans happy with the trade that sent Morgan's counterpart, Tommy Helms, and slugger Lee May to Texas.

Pitcher Jack Billingham and center fielder Cesar Geronimo helped the Reds, but the key to the big deal was Morgan, whose multifaceted game shifted the Big Red Machine into high gear. Morgan became best buddies with Pete Rose, and each of them fed off the other's energy, desire, and baseball savvy. Together at the top of the Reds' batting order, they tormented the league's pitchers by constantly getting on base and running wild. In 1972, his first year with the Reds, Morgan set career highs in batting average (.292), HRs (16), and steals (58); he led the National League in

runs (122) and walks (115); and his on-base percentage exceeded .400 for the first of six consecutive seasons.

It was just the beginning for Joe. The next year he hit 26 HRs, stole 67 bases, and won the first of five consecutive Gold Glove Awards. In the prime of his Reds' career (1973–77), Morgan was a model of consistency, averaging for those five seasons 22 HRs, 109 runs, 118 walks, and 60 stolen bases.

Morgan saved his best for 1975 and '76 when the Reds finally got over the hump and proved they had the stuff of champions. In 1975 he batted .327 and led the league in walks (132) and on-base percentage (.466), all three figures representing career highs. It was also Morgan who got the extra-inning game-winning hit that clinched Game 7 of the 1975 World Series for Cincinnati. Joe was clearly the best all-around player in the NL in 1975, and he won the league MVP Award handily.

When the Reds won another World Championship the next year to affirm their dynastic status, Morgan led the way again. He blasted 27 HRs, knocked in a career-high 111 runs, and led the league in slugging percentage (.576), while stealing 60 bases and scoring 113 runs. He won the 1976 NL MVP Award too, meaning that he was regarded as the best player in the entire league over a two-year period during which the team he led earned the right to call itself the best team in National League history.

After Morgan's great run with the Reds ended in 1979, he finished his career with stints in Houston, San Francisco, Philadelphia, and Oakland. At the time of his retirement, he was third all-time in walks and ninth in stolen bases. Today, when his accomplishments are contemplated, Joe Morgan stands tall as one of the giants of Cooperstown.

YEAR	TM	G	AB	R	H	HR	RBI	SB	BB	SO	BA
1963–71, 1980	HOU (10 yrs)	1032	3729	597	972	72	327	219	678	415	.261
1972–79	CIN (8 yrs)	1154	4008	816	1155	152	612	406	881	410	.288
1981–82	SFG (2 yrs)	224	771	115	208	22	92	38	151	97	.270
1983	PHP (1yr)	123	404	72	93	16	59	18	89	54	.230
1984	OAK (1 yr)	116	365	50	89	6	43	8	66	39	.244
Total		2649	9277	1650	2517	268	1133	689	1865	1015	.271

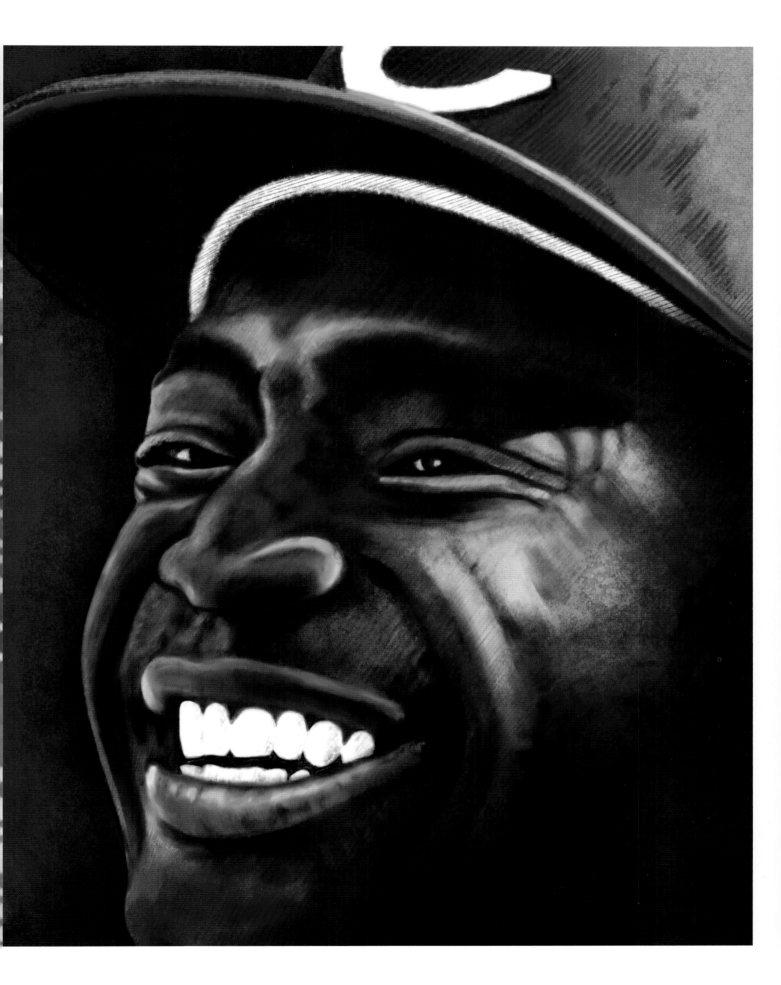

1976–2000

George Foster

The most feared slugger in the National League during his heyday, he is also the most underrated player in Reds' history. Outfielder George Foster is the franchise's single-season "Home Run King," and partly because of his own background he was always overshadowed by the stars of the Big Red Machine.

Born outside Tuscaloosa, Alabama, the shy and sensitive Foster led a sheltered life that ill prepared him for the faster, integrated culture he grew up in once his mother moved the family to Hawthorne, California. Baseball became a means of expression for Foster, but even after he signed with the San Francisco Giants out of El Camino Junior College in the late rounds of the 1968 January draft and earned a promotion to the big leagues by the end of his second year in the minors, he remained introverted and only tenuously confident.

Foster, who was happy playing with his childhood hero, Willie Mays, did not see the opportunity he was being given when the Reds traded for him on May 29, 1971. He became increasingly frustrated at being unable to break into the Reds' starting lineup and entertained thoughts of quitting baseball when he was assigned to Indianapolis to start the 1973 season. The demotion became the turning point of his life as well as his career, as he finally began to believe in himself after putting his faith in God and getting some additional assistance from a hypnotist.

George spent 1974 platooning with Ken Griffey in right field. When Pete Rose moved to third base halfway through the next season, Foster became the regular left fielder, and the Big Red Machine finally shifted into high gear. Foster hit .300 in 1975 in 134 games with 23 home runs and 78 RBI, helping the Reds to their

first World Championship since 1940. It was just the start of big things for him. The next year he batted .306 with 29 homers and 121 RBI, won the MVP Award of the All-Star Game for slamming a three-run HR, and was named *The Sporting News* Player of the Year.

The Reds were blindsided by the Dodgers in 1977, but Foster raised his performance to a whole new level. He became a holy terror at bat, blasting 52 home runs, driving in 149 runs, and totaling 388 bases, all franchise records that still stand today, while averaging .320. Only two players (Hack Wilson and Ralph Kiner) had ever hit more home runs in one National League season, and, like them, Foster racked up his impressive total legitimately, without the aid of performance-enhancing drugs. No one was surprised that George was voted NL MVP for 1977.

In 1978 Foster "slumped" a little, as his stats fell to .281/40/120. He still led the NL in homers and RBI and became only the fourth player in history (along with Ty Cobb, Babe Ruth, and Joe Medwick) to lead his league in RBI three straight years. As the Big Red Machine era came to a close, Foster's stats continued to slip; yet heading into 1982, his first season with the New York Mets to whom he had been traded, he had led both leagues the previous six years in RBI (671) and had been second in homers (198) to Mike Schmidt.

New York with its intense media pressure was the worst place for Foster to move to, and while he was an improvement over what Mets' fans had been used to, he did not turn out to be the franchise's savior. Had he remained in Cincinnati, Foster would have had a better chance at the National Baseball Hall of Fame. He is a most deserving member of the Reds' Valhalla.

YEAR	TM	G	AB	R	H	HR	RBI	SB	BB	SO	BA
1969–71	SFG (3 yrs)	54	129	14	36	4	13	0	8	33	.279
1971–81	CIN (11 yrs)	1253	4454	680	1276	244	861	46	470	882	.286
1982–86	NYM (5 yrs)	655	2389	290	602	99	361	5	185	496	.252
1986	CHW (1 yr)	15	51	2	11	1	4	0	3	8	.216
Total		1977	7023	986	1925	348	1239	51	666	1419	.274

Dave Concepcion

When young Reds' shortstop Davey Concepcion was still a skinny, diffident lightweight at the plate, the veterans in the clubhouse used to kid him mercilessly. "Get lost," they'd say, "we're discussing something you know nothing about: hitting." Concepcion got the message and worked so hard to transform himself into a tough out that when his 19-year Reds' career was over he had accumulated more hits (2,326) than any Reds' player other than Pete Rose and Barry Larkin.

Born June 17, 1948, in Aragua, Venezuela, David Ismael Concepcion grew up idolizing Hall of Fame shortstop and fellow Venezuelan Luis Aparicio. The Reds signed him as a 19-year-old free agent after their Caribbean scouting supervisor noticed him pitching in the Venezuelan National Series for a team sponsored by a bank in Caracas. Concepcion broke in with Tampa in 1967 as a second baseman, but his first manager, George Scherger, shifted him to short and stayed with him even as he struggled to hit .234 for the season.

With Asheville and Indianapolis, the coltish youngster improved enough as a hitter in 1969 that Sparky Anderson made him a Red the following year and worked him into 101 games, often as a late-inning defensive replacement. Concepcion's .260 average belied his readiness though, as he slumped to .205 in 1971 and to .209 in '72 while he shared time at short with three other players.

The winter ball that Concepcion played each off-season in his native country, the encouragement of Scherger, and the hitting instruction of Ted Kluszewski all paid off in 1973 when Davey had a breakout first half. His half season ended on July 22 when he broke his ankle sliding into third base, but before that he had finally established himself as a major-league hitter, batting .287 with eight HRs.

There had never been any doubt about Concepcion's glove. Blessed with sure hands, exceptional range, and a strong and accurate arm, Concepcion was clearly a first-rate shortstop. His replacement for the rest of 1973, veteran Darrel Chaney, said, "In the spring I thought I could beat him out. But he's the best shortstop in the National League now by far. I'll be out there doing a job, but let's not kid anybody. I'm no Davey Concepcion."

With the numbers he posted in 1974 (.281/14/82 and 41 stolen bases in 44 attempts), Concepcion proved that 1973 was no fluke. From 1973 through the 1981 season, he averaged .281, and when he batted .301 in 1978 he became the first Reds' shortstop to hit .300 since 1913. While Concepcion was not a home run hitter, he did flash occasional power and became one of 12 Reds to reach the red seats at Riverfront Stadium when he blasted a big fly off Montreal's Bill Lee on June 9, 1979. He won two Silver Slugger Awards and also gained a reputation as a clutch hitter, leading the team in game-winning RBI (15) in 1976, with five of those coming in one-run games.

As much as Concepcion did to shore up the bottom of the Reds' batting order, his value resided in his steady, often spectacular, fielding. He won five Gold Glove Awards and was a key part of the Big Red Machine's vaunted defensive "strength up the middle."

Davey made nine NL All-Star teams and was voted MVP of the 1982 contest for stroking a two-run homer in the NL's 4–1 victory. Recognizing his leadership and elder statesman's status, the Reds made him captain of the team in 1983. As his career wound down, Concepcion helped groom his replacement, Barry Larkin. Davey received the great honor of having his Reds' number retired in 2007. His boosters remain impatient for his call to Cooperstown.

YEAR	TM	G	AB	R	H	HR	RBI	SB	BB	SO	BA
1970–88	CIN (19 yrs)	2488	8723	993	2326	101	950	321	736	1186	.267

Mario Soto

It's a long way from the poverty of a small town in the Dominican Republic to the pitching mounds of National League ballparks, but Mario Soto made the journey and became the Reds' brightest star during one of the darkest periods in team history.

Soto debuted in pro ball in 1975 with a 2–3 record for Eugene of the Class A Northwest League and then struggled to find his confidence as a major leaguer in the late 1970s, just as the Big Red Machine went into decline. Soto's breakthrough came in the Reds' final game before the 1980 All-Star break. Shouldering an 0–3 record and an ERA hovering near five, Soto relieved rookie starter Bruce Berenyi, who had surrendered six runs to the Houston Astros in one-third of an inning. Soto allowed only three hits over the final 8⅔ innings as the Reds roared back to win 8–6. Used as a long man, a short reliever, and occasionally as a starter, Soto went 9–5 after the break with four saves and an ERA of 2.29. He led the staff in innings pitched (190), finished third in the league in strikeouts, and was the league's toughest pitcher to hit (.187). He also struck out 15 Braves in one game, a high he would repeat in 1982 versus the Mets.

Soto went 12–9 while leading the NL in games started the following, strike-shortened season and then increased his win totals the next three years to 14, 17, and 18 as he established himself as the unquestioned ace of the Reds' staff.

Soto's emergence couldn't have been more timely. His brilliant pitching was one of the few positives in the rock-bottom season of 1982, which saw the Reds lose more than 100 games for the first time in team history, and in the following two campaigns when the Reds lost 88 and 92 games. Relying on a blazing fastball and a devastating changeup, Soto set a new team record for strikeouts in 1982 with 274 and for strikeouts per nine innings (9.57). The 274 Ks were also the most ever by a Latin American pitcher, erasing the record of 264 previously held by Louis Tiant. The strikeouts, combined with the 14 wins and an ERA of 2.79, earned Soto the Reds' pitching Triple Crown in 1982, an honor he copped the next two seasons as well. Soto was so good that Cincinnati sportswriters voted him the team's Outstanding Pitcher *and* Most Valuable Player in 1982 and '83—he also won the Outstanding Pitcher Award in 1980 and '84.

A tough competitor who liked to finish what he started, Soto once told manager Russ Nixon, who'd relieved him with a pitcher who let Soto's 2–1 lead slip away, "I'm not going to pitch eight innings and have that happen. If we're winning, just leave me in." Soto led the NL in complete games twice and totaled 72 complete games over his 12-year career. Mario was also not afraid to pitch inside and instigated all-out brawls on two separate occasions by hitting or brushing back opposing batters.

Soto's status as the Reds' stopper was evident in his receiving a record six Opening Day starting assignments, four of which he won consecutively. He appeared in three All-Star Games and pitched two one-hitters, coming within one strike of a no-hitter against the Atlanta Braves.

When arm problems caused the Reds to release Soto halfway through the 1988 season, he'd rung up 100 victories and 1,449 strikeouts. It was fitting he was inducted into the Reds Hall of Fame with "Long" Bob Ewing, another Reds' pitcher who'd also labored for bad Reds' teams and was much better than his record indicated.

YEAR	TM	W	L	ERA	GS	CG	SHO	IP	H	R	BB	SO
1977–88	CIN (12 yrs)	100	92	3.47	224	72	13	1730.1	1395	732	657	1449

Tom Browning

"Mr. Perfect" is a nickname that only a handful of major-league pitchers have earned. Reds' left-hander Tom Browning entitled himself to the elite moniker when he retired 27 consecutive batters in a 1–0 complete game win over the Los Angeles Dodgers in 1988 at Riverfront Stadium. The rare achievement could not have been turned in by a more fun-loving, down-to-earth, or unlikely candidate, as Browning was a finesse pitcher, not a speedballer.

One of the few natives of Wyoming (Casper) to play big-league baseball, Browning grew up in the small New York towns of Utica and Malone. He was a huge fan of the Big Red Machine and a pretty good high school athlete but did not have the electric stuff to attract much attention from major league scouts who were unimpressed, even after he helped LeMoyne College make two appearances in the Division II College World Series. His big break came when he shut down a highly rated University of Kentucky team while pitching for Tennessee Wesleyan. The Kentucky coach tipped off the Reds, who gave Browning a brief tryout and took him in the ninth round with the 233rd overall pick of the 1982 free-agent draft.

Browning's savvy, pinpoint control, and the screwball he developed while pitching in the Florida Instructional League served him well in the minors, yet the Reds came close to trading him to the St. Louis Cardinals in 1984. The deal was nixed when Reds' general manager Bob Howsam happened to witness Browning throw a no-hitter for AAA Wichita against the Iowa Cubs. In a September call-up that year, Browning made his major league debut under Reds' manager Pete Rose, his boyhood idol.

Browning's 20–9 season in 1985 set a club record for wins by a rookie and dispelled all doubts about his ability to get major league hitters out. Tom was the first rookie since Bob Grim (1954 Yankees) and the first Red since Jim Merritt (1970) to win 20 games. He was named NL Rookie Pitcher of the Year by *The Sporting News* and finished second (behind Vince Coleman) in the Baseball Writers' Association of America (BBWAA) Rookie of the Year voting.

Even as a lack of run support the next season caused his record to slip to 14–13, Browning became the workhorse of the Reds' staff. Fiercely proud of his reliability, he led the NL in games started (39) and would do so three more seasons.

Browning got off to a slow start in 1987 and was demoted to the minors, but he regained his form by the end of the season and turned in his best overall year in '88. He went 18–5, tossed a one-hitter against the Padres on June 6, and then painted his masterpiece against the Dodgers on September 16. In his perfecto, which took less than two hours, the fast-working Browning never went to three balls on a hitter—72 of his 102 pitches were strikes—and the Dodgers never came close to hit all night.

Mr. Perfect won 44 games for the Reds over the following three seasons, and he helped the Reds to their fifth World Championship by winning a game in both the NL Championship Series and the World Series of 1990. Injuries limited his appearances in 1992 and '93, and a broken left arm suffered while he was pitching against San Diego on May 9, 1994, effectively ended his career, despite a comeback attempt with Kansas City.

An enthusiastic prankster, Browning received national attention when he attempted to lift sagging team morale by sitting with fans on the roof of a building outside Wrigley Field during a game in 1993. He retired with 123 wins, 12th all-time among Reds' pitchers.

YEAR	TM	W	L	ERA	GS	CG	SHO	IP	H	R	BB	SO
1984–94	CIN (11 yrs)	123	88	3.92	298	31	12	1911	1918	904	506	997
1995	KCR (1 yr)	0	2	8.10	2	0	0	10	13	9	5	3
Total		123	90	3.94	300	31	12	1921	1931	913	511	1000

Barry Larkin

As a five-year-old, Barry Larkin idolized Superman. As he grew older in the Silverton neighborhood of Cincinnati, he looked up to a couple of real heroes—the Reds' Pete Rose and Dave Concepcion. When Larkin made his major league fairy-tale come-true debut, Rose was the Reds' manager and Concepcion his mentor at the shortstop position. By the time he retired 19 years later, Larkin had become a hero himself, one of baseball's all-time greatest shortstops and gentlemen.

Larkin was born April 28, 1964, into an athletic family headed by hardworking, God-fearing parents who encouraged him not to waste his opportunities. As a University of Michigan Wolverine, Larkin was a two-time All-American and the first to win the Big Ten baseball MVP Award twice. He also played on the 1984 U.S. Olympic team, which won a Silver Medal in Los Angeles. The Reds made him their number one pick in the June 1985 draft and put him on the fast track, but even they were surprised at how quickly he made himself big-league ready. In just his second year in pro ball, Larkin tore up the AAA American Association with Denver in 1986. He batted .329 and was named the league's MVP, even though he played only two-thirds of the season before the Reds brought him up to Cincinnati.

Although Larkin batted .244 during his Reds' tryout, Rose recognized his talent and leadership qualities and was instrumental in the trade of competing shortstop Kurt Stillwell to the Kansas City Royals that cleared the deck for Larkin.

That vote of confidence was all the positive reinforcement that Larkin needed. He not only solidified his status as a major-league regular in 1988 but also enjoyed a breakout season. He batted .296, went more than two games without a hit only once, and was the toughest batter in the majors to strike out, whiffing only 24 times in 652 appearances. He was named to the National League All-Star team (his first of 12 selections), made *The Sporting News*'s postseason All-Star team, and won a Silver Slugger Award as the best hitting shortstop in the NL.

An injury the day before the All-Star Game limited Larkin to 97 games in 1989, but his career-high .342 batting average for the season showed what heights he was capable of scaling. Larkin went on to hit over .300 eight more times; he won three Gold Gloves and eight more Silver Slugger Awards; he became the first Red and first shortstop ever to hit five home runs in two consecutive games in 1991; and in 1996 he became the first shortstop to hit 30 or more home runs and steal 30 or more bases in the same season. By mid-career Larkin was widely recognized as one of baseball's most complete players, and opposing managers often named him as the player they would choose if they were starting a team from scratch.

As impressive as these accomplishments were, the highlights of Larkin's career were the times he helped the Reds win. In 1990 Larkin led the Reds to a shocking four-game sweep over the highly favored Oakland A's in the Reds' first World Series since 1976. The local BBWAA named Larkin the MVP of that illustrious team. Then in 1995 Barry won the MVP Award of the National League, even though the Reds were ousted from postseason play in the NL Championship Series by the Atlanta Braves.

By the time injuries and age caught up to Larkin, everyone realized that Barry had put together a Hall of Fame career. He received baseball's ultimate honor in only his third year on the ballot and entered baseball's Valhalla with the third-most home runs and fourth-most stolen bases among Hall of Fame shortstops.

YEAR	TM	G	AB	R	H	HR	RBI	SB	BB	SO	BA
1986–2004	CIN (19 yrs)	2180	7937	1329	2340	198	960	379	939	817	.295

Eric Davis

In terms of raw natural ability, center fielder Eric Keith Davis may have been the most talented athlete to ever play for the Cincinnati Reds. Injuries prevented him from sustaining the elite level of performance he displayed in numerous bursts of greatness, but no one could question his courage and resilience after he'd made not one but two remarkable comebacks. He felt underappreciated but realized how much Reds' fans admired him when he was inducted into the team's Hall of Fame in 2005, just four years after retiring.

The Eric Davis story started May 29, 1962, in the rough South Central neighborhood of Los Angeles, California. Good parents with Christian values helped Davis stay focused on sports and away from the surrounding drug and gang culture. In high school he was such a star in basketball and baseball that his being taken by the Reds in the eighth round of the 1980 draft was a disappointment.

Davis started slowly in the minors but began developing swiftly after he was switched from shortstop, his high school position, to center field. A hot start in 1984 at Wichita earned the youngster a promotion to Cincinnati, where Dave Parker took him under his wing. His .224 average in 57 games was offset by the blanketing defensive coverage of the outfield he provided and the power potential hinted at in his blasting home runs (five total) in four straight September games.

This tantalizing debut was curtailed by injury, a sequence that became the frustrating pattern to Davis's career. Slender and muscular, the six-foot-three, 185-pound Davis, with his 30-inch waist and 16-inch biceps, had a powerful body that enabled him to motor around the diamond like a sports car, launch baseballs into upper-deck orbit, and make leaping, home run-nullifying catches high above outfield walls. Unfortunately, that body was unable to hold up under Davis's punishing, all-out style of play.

Because of injuries, Davis would never play in more than 135 games in a season, and the postseason surgery he underwent in 1984 would be merely the first of eight operations in seven years.

When healthy, Davis was a marvel who could carry a team for weeks, even months, at a time. In his first full year with the Reds, in 1986, he hit 27 home runs and stole 80 bases in 415 at bats. The next season he had the best year of his career (.293/37/100) with 50 steals and 120 runs scored, all in 129 games. In his prime (1986–90), he was the game's greatest dual threat, averaging 30 HRs and 40 steals.

The 1990 World Series was the highlight and nadir of his career. His two-run homer in his first Series at bat set the tone for the Reds' sweep of the favored Oakland A's, but the lacerated kidney injury he suffered attempting a diving catch in Game 4 nearly ended his career. His next four seasons with the Reds, Dodgers, and Tigers were all subpar because of the lingering effects of the kidney injury and a spinal injury suffered when he ran into the wall at Fenway Park.

The worn-down Davis retired, but after sitting out all of 1995 he came back with the Reds and turned in an amazing year (.287/26/83). His second comeback was even more inspiring.

Midway through the 1997 season with Baltimore, Davis was diagnosed with colon cancer, which required immediate and radical surgery. He came back from that ordeal to hit a game-winning HR in the AL Championship Series and to finish fourth the next year in the race for the AL batting title with the best average of his career: .327. He became a hero and role model, not merely a terrific ballplayer.

YEAR	TM	G	AB	R	H	HR	RBI	SB	BB	SO	BA
1984–91, 1996	CIN (9 yrs)	985	3272	635	886	203	615	270	494	874	.271
1992–93	LAD (2 yrs)	184	643	78	149	19	85	52	77	159	.232
1993–94	DET (2 yrs)	60	195	33	41	9	28	7	32	63	.210
1997–98	BAL (2 yrs)	173	610	110	196	36	114	13	58	155	.321
1999–00	STL (2 yrs)	150	445	65	126	11	70	6	66	109	.283
2001	SFG (1 yr)	74	156	17	32	4	22	1	13	38	.205
Total		1626	5321	938	1430	282	934	349	740	1398	.269

Sean Casey

When you trade the pitcher scheduled to be your Opening Day starter the day before the big game, as the Reds did on March 30, 1998, you'd better know what you're doing. Brassy Reds' general manager Jim Bowden did know, and he didn't fret over the howls resulting from the swap of veteran right-hander Dave Burba to Cleveland for an unknown minor-league first baseman. "Reds' fans will love Sean Casey," he predicted confidently.

Boy, was Bowden right about Sean Thomas Casey, a Willingboro, New Jersey, native who'd grown up in the Pittsburgh area. Casey rolled into town like a revivalist, preaching an infectious brand of cheerfulness, gregariousness, and kindness, all of it genuine, and soon converted not only skeptical Reds' fans but all of Cincinnati to become one of the City's most beloved adopted sons.

It helped, of course, that Casey could rip line drives with his eyes closed, unlike his Mudville namesake. He'd won an NCAA Division 1 batting championship at the University of Richmond in 1995, and after batting .386 for Akron and .361 for Buffalo in '97 he'd been named the number one prospect in the entire Indians' organization.

Casey's bright future with his new team almost ended before it started, when his right eye socket was shattered in a batting practice accident before the Reds' third game of the '98 season. He made a full recovery, and miraculously his vision even improved. He played 27 games in Indianapolis while rehabbing and managed to hit .272 in 96 games for the Reds.

The next year Casey became the regular first baseman and cemented his status as a Cincinnati Reds legend. He blistered the ball at a .332 clip (fourth best in the NL), led the league in extra-base hits with 66, and chalked up 25 homers and 99 ribbies, becoming the first Reds'

first baseman since Tony Perez with at least 25 HRs and 90 RBI. He made a major contribution to the Reds' surprising turnaround (a 19-win improvement over the previous season) and bid for the postseason, which ended in a one-game playoff loss to the New York Mets.

Casey slipped a little in succeeding years, although he batted over .300 four more times for Cincinnati and led the team in batting six out of his seven full seasons with the Reds. He also led the Reds in hits four times, in doubles three times, and in runs and RBI twice. He was a NL All-Star three times and nearly duplicated his big 1999 season in 2004 when he compiled stats of .324/24/99.

What never diminished was the big Irishman's enthusiasm and concern for others. No one ever saw Casey, dubbed "the Mayor of Riverfront Stadium," turn down an autograph request from a kid; he donated generously to various charities; and a 2007 *Sports Illustrated* poll named him "the friendliest player in baseball" in a landslide.

In December 2005 Casey was traded to the Pittsburgh Pirates, who moved him to Detroit halfway through the 2006 season. In the postseason that year for the Tigers, he was sensational: batting .353 against the Yankees, .333 against the A's, and, in the World Series, .529 against the St. Louis Cardinals; for a composite postseason average of .432. He batted .296 the next year in his last full season, and he ended his career playing 69 games for the 2008 Red Sox, while batting .322. Overall, Casey finished with a .302 batting average, 1,531 hits, 130 HR, 735 RBI, and an on-base percentage of .371. Upon Sean's induction into the Reds Hall of Fame, Hal McCoy spoke for Reds' fans everywhere in describing him "as the nicest person to play major league baseball. Ever."

YEAR	TM	G	AB	R	H	HR	RBI	SB	BB	SO	BA
1997	CLE (1 yr)	6	10	1	2	0	1	0	1	2	.200
1998–05	CIN (8 yrs)	1075	4007	588	1223	118	604	15	387	465	.305
2006	PIT (1 yr)	59	213	30	63	3	29	0	23	22	.296
2006–07	DET (2 yrs)	196	637	57	179	9	84	2	49	63	.281
2008	BOS (1 yr)	69	199	14	64	0	17	1	17	25	.322
Total		1405	5066	690	1531	130	735	18	477	577	.302

Ken Griffey Jr.

Like father, like son. Only better. That's the Ken Griffey Jr. story in a nutshell. And it's an implausible tale because the father was so good!

Ken Griffey Sr. was a fast, line-drive hitting outfielder who played 12 of his 19 major-league seasons in Cincinnati. As a key member of the Big Red Machine, he batted at the top of the order, setting the table for the Reds' big guns. Griffey made three All-Star teams and batted .300 for the Reds five times, with a high of .336 in 1976. He retired with 2,143 hits and a lifetime average of .296. That's a proud record that anybody would be hard-pressed to better; but for "Junior," as Griffey's son was often called, it was like teeing off on batting practice meatballs.

Born, like his dad and Stan Musial, in Donora, Pennsylvania, Griffey cut his baseball teeth in the Reds' Riverfront Stadium clubhouse. By the time he was a senior at Cincinnati's Archbishop Moeller High School, his sweet left-handed swing had scouts everywhere swooning. The Seattle Mariners took him with the first overall pick of the 1987 amateur draft, and two years later "The Kid" was in the major leagues. Griffey Senior ended his career in Seattle, and father and son played 51 games together during the 1990–91 seasons. On September 14, 1990, they became the first such combination to hit back-to-back homers in the major leagues.

It was immediately obvious that Griffey was an immense baseball talent. He made the American League All-Star team in his second season (1990) and for the next nine years. While Junior hit for average, the ball simply jumped off his bat, and he became one of the premier power hitters in the game. He hit 40+ HRs six times and led the league in homers four times, including 1997 and '98 when he blasted 56 taters each season. He knocked in 100+ runs seven times and more than 140 runs three times, and his slugging percentage surpassed .600 five times. He won the AL MVP Award in 1997 when he batted .304 and led the league in home runs, RBI (147), runs (125), slugging percentage (.646), and total bases (393). He did all this heavy hitting while also making numerous spectacular catches, which earned him the Gold Glove Award for the AL's best fielding center fielder for 10 consecutive years (1990–99).

In February 2000 Griffey was traded from Seattle to Cincinnati, thrilling Reds' fans who'd felt that Junior had belonged to them all along. Griffey started slowly in 2000 but rallied to bat .271 with 40 HRs and 118 RBI. The next four years were frustrating and disappointing, as injuries ended Griffey's season prematurely three times, and he was able to play on average only 79 games a year, averaging 16 HRs and 43 RBI.

In 2005 the 35-year-old Griffey mustered the strength to put together his second-best season for the Reds, batting .301 with 35 HRs and 92 RBI, good enough to earn him the NL Comeback Player of the Year Award. He slipped in 2006 (.252/27/72), rebounded a bit in 2007 (.277/30/93), and then, after being traded in 2008 to the Chicago White Sox, played out the string back in Seattle.

Because of injuries and aging, Griffey was not the dominating player in Cincinnati that he had been in Seattle, yet during his nine years in Cincinnati he set many records and reached numerous career milestones, such as his 500th home run, which was also career hit 2,143, the exact number hit by his father. His 630 career homers, untainted by the use of performance-enhancing drugs, make him a first ballot shoo-in for the Hall of Fame in Cooperstown.

YEAR	TM	G	AB	R	H	HR	RBI	SB	BB	SO	BA
1989–99 2009–10	SEA (13 yrs)	1685	6317	1113	1843	417	1216	167	819	1081	.292
2000–2008	CIN (9 yrs)	945	3353	533	904	210	602	17	476	673	.270
2008	CHW (1 yr)	41	131	16	34	3	18	0	17	25	.260
Total		2671	9801	1662	2781	630	1836	184	1312	1779	.284

Brandon Phillips

After the close of the Big Red Machine era, the Reds saw a succession of sparkling second basemen come and go: Ron Oester, Mariano Duncan, Bip Roberts, Bret Boone, Pokey Reese. Searching for a new candidate to continue this heritage, they located a brash young southern kid brimming with unfulfilled potential, and to get him they went north, picking the pocket of their intrastate rivals, the Cleveland Indians. The bargain basement steal has been better than anyone dared to dream, so good that he is poised to surpass even the great Joe Morgan as the Reds' all-time leader at the position in every meaningful statistical category, save one (stolen bases).

Born June 28, 1981, in Raleigh, North Carolina, Brandon Emil Phillips grew up in the Atlanta, Georgia, area where he became a big fan of Barry Larkin. A 1999 second-round draft pick of the Montreal Expos, he was rated in 2002 as the top prospect in the organization. He went to Cleveland in a mid-year trade and following the season was named the best prospect in the Indians' organization.

Phillips's fast-track progress then came to a screeching halt. Given the Indians' second-base job in 2003, he hit .208 in 112 games and was returned to the minors. After giving Brandon only 31 major-league at bats over the next two years, the Tribe lost faith in him and unloaded him on the Reds for a player to be named later.

Whether it was simply the fresh start or the way Reds' fans took him into their hearts, the 25-year-old Phillips immediately became the player the talent evaluators had foreseen.

He earned NL Player of the Week honors in the latter part of April for hitting .452 with three HRs and 17 RBI, becoming the first Red since 1979 to have that many ribbies in one week. For the season Phillips batted .276 with 17 HRs and 75 RBI, and he led the team in hits and multi-hit games.

Phillips's encore in 2007 showed what a special player he could be. While batting .288 with 94 RBI, he led the Reds in hits again (187), walloped 30 HRs, and swiped 33 bases, becoming only the third 30–30 player in franchise history. A free swinger with a wide stance, Phillips loves to pull the ball but is also capable of spraying it to all fields. While he hit from all nine spots in the batting order during his first eight years with the Reds, he has batted most often (527 games) in the cleanup spot. He led the Reds in RBI in 2009 with 98 and in 2013 with a career-high 103.

Phillips's glove has been even better than his bat. He won his first of four Gold Glove Awards in 2008 when he enjoyed a 78-game errorless streak and led the league in fielding percentage (.990), making only seven errors in 706 chances. Acrobatic, inventive plays involving perfect behind-the-back and between-the-legs throws have become his specialty and have left many a stunned broadcaster near speechless. "I surprise myself sometimes," he said in awe of his penchant for making great plays.

What has most endeared Phillips to Reds' fans is his million-watt, always switched-on smile, his irrepressible love of the game, and his willingness—yea eagerness—to interact with his supporters. Phillips was quick to use social media to stay connected to his fans, and by the end of the 2013 season he had almost a million followers on Twitter. *Cincinnati Magazine* called him the "most entertaining player in baseball," and manager Dusty Baker said he's already a shoo-in for the Reds Hall of Fame and possibly on his way to Cooperstown. Phillips's fans would not argue with either assessment.

YEAR	TM	G	AB	R	H	HR	RBI	SB	BB	SO	BA
2002–05	CLE (4 yrs)	135	432	43	89	6	38	4	19	92	.206
2006–13	CIN (8 yrs)	1204	4751	690	1318	160	666	155	308	710	.277
Total		1339	5183	733	1407	166	704	159	327	802	.271

Joey Votto

The Reds have always been able to find or produce a cornerstone player when they needed him most. After the retirement of Barry Larkin and the departure of Sean Casey, the team was desperate for such a talent once again. Riding to the rescue in 2007 was Canadian Joey Votto, a once-in-a-generation player who has overcome adversity and injury to become the face of the franchise and one of the most consistently great hitters in the game.

Born September 10, 1983, in Toronto, the left-handed hitting Votto was the Reds' second pick in the 2002 draft out of high school (Richview Collegiate Institute). Carrying a copy of Ted Williams's *The Science of Hitting* with him, Votto played and hit well at every stop in the Reds' farm system on his way to the big leagues. In 2006 he was named the Reds' Minor League Player of the Year for winning the Southern League's batting championship and MVP Award. After showing with Triple-A Louisville that he had nothing left to prove in the minors, Votto was called up to Cincinnati on September 1, 2007. He homered in his second at bat and hit .321 over his 24-game baptism.

Votto began the 2008 season platooning with veteran Scott Hatteberg but quickly became the Reds' regular first sacker and three-hole hitter. Joey wound up playing in 151 games and breaking Frank Robinson's team record for RBI by a rookie. He also led National League rookies in batting average (.297), hits, home runs, on-base percentage, slugging percentage, total bases, and multi-hit games. Somehow he finished second in the Rookie of the Year balloting to Cubs' catcher Geovany Soto.

Votto was a holy terror during the first two months of the next season, but on May 30, 2009, while batting .357, he went on the disabled list and did not return to the Reds' lineup until June 23. In his three-week absence, it was revealed that he had been suffering from severe depression and anxiety caused by his father's sudden death the previous August at age 52. After getting the help he needed to cope with his grief, Votto reset his laserlike focus and finished the year batting .322, fifth best in the NL. He was named Player of the Week September 21–27 for hitting 10 doubles in a five-game span, a feat not done since 1932.

In 2010 Votto put it all together, batting .324 (second best in the league) with 37 HRs and 113 RBI to become the 10th Red to win the NL MVP Award. He also made his first NL All-Star team as the overwhelming favorite of the fans in an online balloting to determine the final roster spot and has been on the team every year since.

The next year Votto hit only 29 HRs but led the league in doubles (40) and became the first Red since 1985–86 to enjoy back-to-back 100+ RBI seasons. Votto hurt his knee while sliding on June 29 and missed more than two weeks of the 2012 season, but he recovered to post another fine average of .337.

Votto received some criticism for driving in only 73 runs in 2013, but by then he had established his value to the team as the type of rare hitter who combines high average with high on-base percentage. His refusal to swing at bad pitches in an attempt to drive in more runs resulted in his leading the league in walks three straight years (2011–13) and in on-base percentage four straight years (2010–13). Satisfied with his approach, the Reds gave Votto the fourth-biggest contract in baseball history. Reds' fans are ecstatic that he is signed through the 2023 season.

YEAR	TM	G	AB	R	H	HR	RBI	SB	BB	SO	BA
2007–13	CIN (7 yrs)	890	3180	529	999	157	530	47	564	700	.314